Ute Tales

Ute Tales

Collected by Anne M. Smith, assisted by Alden Hayes

Foreword by Joseph Jorgensen

University of Utah Press
Salt Lake City

Volume Twenty-nine of the University of Utah

Publications in the American West

The paper in this book meets the standards for permanence
and durability established by the Committee on Production
Guidelines for Book Longevity of the Council on Library Re-
sources

Library of Congress Cataloging-in-Publication Data

Ute tales / collected by Anne M. Smith, assisted by Alden
    Hayes ; foreword by Joseph G. Jorgensen.
        p. cm. — (University of Utah publications in the
    American West ; v. 29)
      ISBN 0-87480-442-6 (alk. paper)
      1. Ute Indians—Legends. I. Smith, Anne M. (Anne
    Milne), 1900–1981. II. Hayes, Alden C. III. Series.
    E99.U8U855 1992
    398.2′089974—dc20   92-53607
                                                                CIP

Contents

Foreword

As a Yale University graduate student in anthropology, Anne M. Smith first visited the Northern Utes of the Uinta and Ouray Reservation in eastern Utah during the summer of 1936. Nan, as Anne was known, returned in the summer of 1937.[1] The anthropology faculty at Yale in the late 1930s was graced by several luminaries of the discipline: Edward Sapir, the famed ethnolinguist; Leslie Spier, the comparativist and fine ethnographer of American Indian culture; and George Peter Murdock, America's preeminent student of comparative social structure.

Nan was interested in ethnology, about how Indian culture once was, but she was particularly interested in contemporary Indian culture and the forces that had affected Indian societies since first Contact. She pursued that interest through most of her adult professional life, and whenever possible she used her professional skills to assist Indians. Among Nan's early professional advocacies of Indians was her contribution to the famous Confederated Bands of Ute Indians case, which was heard before the Indian Claims Commission in the late 1940s.[2] The Ute case was the first to be heard by the Commission and resulted in a $31.8 million judgment to the Ute Indians of Utah and Colorado (Northern Utes, Southern Utes, and Ute Mountain Utes) for land expropriated from them in Colorado in the nineteenth century.

During the first five decades of this century it was rare for faculty or graduate students to express interest in contemporary Indian life. Nan's teachers were more concerned with reconstructing the languages and cultures of North America's native peoples as they were at first Contact and accounting for how they came to be that way. Nan's primary mentors, Spier and Sapir, neither studied nor published about the contemporary economies, social organizations, or political affairs of the people with whom they worked, nor did they seek to account for the forces that affected contemporary Indian societies during the period they were among them.

Like her mentors, Nan sought information from elderly informants to assist in reconstructing Ute culture in the "ethnographic present"—its subsistence economy, technology, social and kinship organization, religious practices, band organization, and distribution just prior to protracted influences from Europe. She was not insensitive to the differences between the Ute culture she sought to reconstruct and the Ute culture she observed, however. Nan was appalled at much of what she saw in the relations between whites and Utes in the Uinta Basin. But in 1936 and 1937, as a fledgling anthropologist studying Ute mythology, she was not prepared to analyze white-Indian relations, or the political economy of the Uinta Basin and the niche occupied by Ute Indians.

Northern Utes in the Mid-1930s

I resist a comprehensive summary of Ute contact history, but some summary is necessary to understand the Northern Ute context in the mid-1930s. Suffice it to say that land occupied and used by the Northern Utes had been reduced from about 70 million acres in 1860 to 4 million acres in 1905 to 360,000 acres in 1937. This marked the lifetimes of many living Utes, including the majority of Nan's informants. Of 113,000 acres allotted in severalty to Northern Utes between 1905 and 1907 pursuant to the General Allotment Act of 1887, about 30,000 acres (26 percent) had been alienated by 1934 when the Indian Reorganization Act was passed and alienation terminated.[3]

In 1906, soon after the bulk of Uinta and White River lands were allotted and all but 250,000 unallotted acres placed in the public domain, the Uinta Irrigation Project (UIP) was begun by the Bureau of Indian Affairs (BIA). The project had been rejected by Utes, but desired by the BIA and white, predominantly Mormon, settlers who claimed the unallotted Indian lands. The goal of this project was to make family farming successful.[4] Over the next thirty years the federal government allocated well over $2 million for the project. Indian allottees and heirs incurred debts against their allotments to repay the federal government, whether or not they desired the UIP, and whether or not they raised crops or livestock on their allotments. The primary beneficiaries of the UIP were whites who had homesteaded or purchased Indian land placed in the public domain after allotment, or had leased Indian land.

In 1904 the Uinta and Ouray Ute Indian reservations encompassed nearly the entire Uinta Basin,[5] portions of the Uinta Mountains to the north, and the Tavaputs Plateau stretching more than a hundred miles to the south of the agency town of Fort Duchesne. By 1936 the Uinta and Ouray reservations had been consolidated as a tiny remnant, encompassed by several non-Indian farming and ranching communities. Even the reservation was a patchwork of Indian and non-Indian property. The communities that surrounded it had sprung up after 1906 when Ute reservation lands were expropriated by the federal government.

The earliest settlers sought Uinta Irrigation Project water, and also to impound water on former reservation land before it crossed the reservation, thereby establishing prior use rights under Utah law. By 1923 the white interlopers had begun a concerted effort to develop the Uinta Basin. They lobbied state and federal governments to develop roads and water containment and diversion projects that would assist local agriculture, extraction of timber, and mining projects. A Uinta Basin Industrial Convention (UBIC) was formed, which sponsored annual meetings whose conclusion each year was highlighted by a parade, a pageant, and a dance. Nan Smith attended this affair during her first field visit in August of 1936 because the UBIC planners had announced that among their many accomplishments was the understanding of the Indian. UBIC literature asked rhetorically, "Was the Indian with his legends, crafts and folklore better understood?" Nan's notes say, "The UBIC was the most blatantly segregated event I have ever witnessed. . . . The dancing at night was for whites only. In 1937 I skipped it, and went to Salt Lake City."

In 1936, about 67 percent of all allotments were snarled in heirship disputes. Ute allottees and heirs were being assessed by the BIA for maintenance charges relative to the UIP, and by the state of Utah for irrigation water. So, whether or not an allottee or joint heirs farmed, indebtedness automatically accrued from UIP costs. Moreover, landowners who did not pay off their irrigation debts could not farm.[6]

A few extended families ran cattle and sheep, although there was little surplus for market sales. Utes contributed to their own subsistence by raising and consuming cattle and sheep, leasing or selling their allotments to whites, working for the federal government—averaging about 10 percent full-time employment—or, on a temporary basis, working for white ranchers and farmers during haying and cutting seasons, and by hunting deer, elk, rabbits, and sage hens, fishing, and collecting nuts and berries. The federal government provided assistance with rations.

At that time, about 40 percent of Northern Ute houses had dirt floors. Most houses with flooring were either frame or clapboard shacks which were invariably overcrowded. About 30 percent of all Utes suffered from either tuberculosis or trachoma, each of which is associated with poor diets and dank, dark living conditions. Tuberculosis, pneumonia, and several gastrointestinal diseases were the major causes of death.

Most adult Utes were illiterate. Literate adults had seldom attended school beyond the eighth grade.

Many of Nan's field notes mention living conditions in 1936 and 1937. The comments are usually rather pithy. "The whole family were still eating when I got there, so I sat down by the stove and took out my knitting. You can't imagine anything much more poverty stricken or any dirtier than that house. It was warm, however, and that was something. . . .

Yet, while noting abject living conditions, and being appalled by the poverty she witnessed, Ute families impressed her with their humor. Nan's central interests were in Ute myths, about which we will say more later, so it is not surprising that her comments on housing, diet, social structure, and politics are not main features in her daily journal. Yet, from her descriptions of raconteurs and the joy with which stories were told and stories were heard, it is evident that coping with adverse conditions was not an everyday topic within Ute households, nor was it a principal theme in the myths she was told.

Between Nan's first and second field trips to the Uinta and Ouray Reservation, the Northern Utes ratified a tribal constitution and charter under provisions of the Indian Reorganization Act of 1934. Only 30 percent of eligible voters ratified the charter, but the vote was sufficient (any simple majority would suffice to ratify an IRA constitution or charter, including 1 for and 0 against). The charter allowed for the establishment of a business committee to conduct the economic, legislative, and judicial affairs of the tribe but gave veto power over any and all decisions to the Secretary of Interior.

There is some evidence that ratification was greatly influenced by local BIA officials who turned out favorable votes among the mixed-bloods and Uncompaghre full-bloods. The first committeemen to be elected were mixed-bloods and Uncompaghre full-bloods. Their actions created considerable animosity among the White River and Uinta full-bloods, who had scores of disputes to settle with both groups, and between full-blood Uncompaghres and mixed-bloods.[7]

During Nan's second field trip in 1937, at the depths of the Great Depression, it was time for Ute property owners to pay for the services and improvements to the irrigation system. Ditches and canals had been dug, individual allotments had been leveled and plowed, water had been diverted. Few Utes could pay the debts against their allotments or inherited land. Some lots had accrued as much as $1,600 in debts against them.

The tribal business committee, which was formed about the time Nan returned to Utah, began administering tribal political and economic affairs. The committee's authority was restricted by provisions in the IRA which delegated authority over financial expenditures and jural punishments to the BIA, Congress, and the Secretary of Interior. One of the committee's first acts was to draw $100,000, made available as a revolving credit loan by the IRA, and $100,000 from tribal funds to purchase allotments, whether or not in heirship, as a means of settling old expenditures and Congress-authorized purchases.[8] The business committee had no real power. The BIA hatched the plan to use tribal loans and tribal funds to pay off debts. The business committee followed the BIA's plan and began coercing allottees to sell. The tribal corporate body's leadership was using tribal funds to settle old debts incurred by individual tribal members. The abuse did not go unnoticed.

During Nan's tenure on the reservation, Northern Utes were paying debts they had not wished to incur, with Ute funds over which they had no control, to the Ute tribe. The debtors never touched the money as the tribe bought back Indian land from Indians and used Indian money to do it, and the business committee used tribal and federal funds to purchase acreage that was being liquidated by bankrupt white entrepreneurs.

Nan attended one of several meetings held in various

reservation communities and called by the Superintendent to air issues and inform Utes about decisions the Commissioner (John Collier) had made regarding tribal problems. These problems included debts incurred from the irrigation project, the purchase of allotment lands, the cession of white-owned lands, and so forth. Most of the discussion by Utes was conducted in the Ute language. Nan did not understand all the topics discussed, let alone the language. Thorough understanding would require much time, knowledge of the Ute language, and knowledge of the economic and political issues affecting the tribe, including band factionalism and mixed-blood/full-blood factionalism. Yet Nan's unpublished field notes demonstrate that she was impressed by the dignity and knowledge of several Utes who spoke to the issue before them and the attention accorded the speakers by Utes who had crowded into the room. Among related topics, the speakers made a pitch to limit the use of Ute funds by the newly formed business committee, to remove whites by land cessions from erstwhile reservation land, to acquire more grazing land for the Utes, and to control Uinta Irrigation Project canals for Indian use. According to Nan's notes, the behavior of the Utes soon changed when

> old —— went on endlessly, finally degenerating into a whine that the Govt. should hand out some of the tribal moneys to the old people who wouldn't be here much longer to enjoy it, and the old people were broke supporting their kids. The audience got restless and paid little attention to him, they talked, made comments, did some of the noisiest throat clearing, and even —— started to shout something, but —— shushed her. I asked her what —— said and she replied, "Just being funny." After the meeting was over everybody gathered in the store for pop and ice cream cones.

No matter how serious the occasion, there is always room for levity. Lengthy orations, per se, are not ridiculed,

nor are orations that seek to benefit elderly Utes. But be-
seeching the government to benefit a few, rather than all,
and subordinating long-term tribal concerns for the momen-
tary concerns of a few, also, is not good form among the
Utes. Utes are not bashful critics. If the continuing debates
over the use of tribal funds from 1948 through today are a
reasonable indication of past opinions, the old man's message
was undoubtedly an accurate description of the desires of
many elderly Utes in 1937, not his alone.

The issues discussed at the meetings in 1937 festered
through the 1960s, erupting variously in a protracted fight
over the rightful governance of Ute bands, fights over the ra-
cial composition of the business committee, fights over the
disposition of funds won in several land claims judgments in
the 1950s and early 1960s, and discussions leading to the termination proceedings of 1954.[9]

Nan Smith and Ute Tales

Soon after her second field trip and before completing
her doctoral dissertation, Nan published a short piece on the
Northern Utes ("The Northern Ute," *American Anthropologist* 40:627–30, 1938). Almost thirty-five years slipped by
before Nan published her *Ethnography of the Northern Utes*.[10]
By the time she was ready to return to work on her massive
Great Basin mythology, her husband, East, died; she was
slowed by emphysema and a broken wrist; and her attention
was diverted by political issues requiring her attention. Still,
she was not so slowed that she had to forgo her summer trips
to Martha's Vineyard to swim in the surf and share her life
with her good friends, Beatrice and John Whiting and Cora
Dubois. And she found time to travel to the Sea of Cortez for
swimming vacations and discussions with her friend Frances
Swadesh.

It was during the period in which she prepared her ethnographic field notes from 1936–39 for publication that I be-

came her friend, eventually her literary executor. When Nan first contacted me I was finishing my *Sun Dance Religion*, which analyzes the causes and the retention of the Sun Dance religion among Utes and Shoshones, and she was trying to locate a copy of my tedious doctoral dissertation on Northern Ute ethnohistory and culture change.

Nan asked me to read her draft manuscript of the *Ethnography*. Upon completing it, I told Nan I had been a fan of hers since borrowing her whopping doctoral dissertation (Anne M. Cooke [Smith], *An Analysis of Basin Mythology*, 2 vols., 1939) from the Yale University library. I suggested that her dissertation shouldn't languish in the stacks at Yale. The myths were so rich and so frequently humorous and the Great Basin mythologic area so unique that the entire dissertation should appear in a form available to her informants' great-grandchildren and great-great-grandchildren, and indeed to all of us. In addition, I told her, the paper in the copy of the dissertation I had borrowed from Yale more than a decade earlier was so fragile and the carbon so faint that her dissertation would be but a title in the card catalogue in a few years.[11]

Nan's dissertation tackles a problem that would interest very few contemporary graduate students or their advisors. In 1935 her mentors, Leslie Spier and Edward Sapir, suggested to Nan that little was known of the Great Basin, particularly about Basin mythology, even though Sapir, J. Alden Mason, Alfred L. Kroeber, and Robert H. Lowie had collected a few tales during visits to various Basin communities during the first few decades of this century. Julian Steward's monumental *Basin-Plateau Sociopolitical Organization* was not published by the Bureau of American Ethnology at the Smithsonian Institution until 1938, so little was known of the aboriginal societies of this vast intermontane sink stretching from the Sierra to the Rockies, and from the Snake to the Colorado rivers.

Spier's interest was motivated by several factors. He wanted to ensure that a large corpus of Paviotso (Northern

Paiute), Shoshone, and Ute–Southern Paiute tales were collected before there were no living raconteurs to tell them.[12]
This was a commonly shared concern of American eth-
nologists in the years before World War II. Spier wanted Nan
to determine whether the Basin formed a mythological area.
That is to say, he wanted to know whether the corpuses of
lore told in the many Basin societies were more similar
among Basin societies than between Basin societies and
societies outside the Basin. The analysis of similarities and
differences in required analyses of plots, characters, and
types of lore before comparisons could be made. This is
rigorous, arduous stuff. Nan was up to it. She wanted to answer the questions Spier posed, and she did.

When Nan Smith arrived at the Uinta and Ouray Reservation in Fort Duchesne, Utah, in 1936, she had been
forewarned by the published comments of Alfred Kroeber
("Ute Tales," *Journal of American Folklore* 14:252–86,
1901), J. Alden Mason ("Myths of the Uinta Utes," *Journal
of American Folklore* 23:299–363, 1910), and her teacher,
Edward Sapir ("Notes on Northern Utes," unpublished,
1909) that it was difficult to secure ethnographic information
from Northern Utes. Nan was not surprised when her initial
experiences were similar to those of earlier ethnographers
among the Utes and saw no reason, given the nature of Ute-
white contacts during the previous century why "Utes should
trust whites" (Smith 1974:8). By the end of her first research
session, however, Nan had made several good contacts,
gaining the trust of more than twenty-five informants. These
persons assisted her again in 1937.

In 1936 and 1937 Nan collected several hundred tales
among raconteurs from the three Northern Ute bands: Uinta
(the inhabitants of central and eastern Utah prior to 1847),
White River (the pre-reservation inhabitants of the Yampa
River and White River areas of Colorado), and Uncompaghre
(erstwhile inhabitants of the Gunnison River area of Colorado).[13] To determine whether the lore of Utes was similar to
the lore of the residents of the central Great Basin was part

of Nan's challenge. She had to collect many more myths than the 102 published here. And she had to collect them from Shoshone and Paviotso raconteurs as well. She collected them, more than seven hundred in all, and she went on to compare the tales she collected with tales collected from raconteurs on the Plains, in the Plateau, in California, and in the Southwest.[14] Her analysis of those tales appears in the first volume of her dissertation. The problem she tackled was not trivial, nor was the solution obvious.

When Nan embarked on her study, the evidence suggested that the precursors of Northern Utes, and their congeners on reservations in southern Colorado, had been denizens of the mountains from the Wasatch on the west through the Rockies on the East for several centuries prior to 1936. They were robust and daring horse thiefs by the early 18th century, and spectacular equestrian big game hunters with huge horse herds by the early 19th century. How, possibly, could Utes with so exciting a past be similar to the tribes of the Great Basin proper? Those people, from the fringes of the Great Salt Lake to the fringes of Owens Lake in California, had spent several centuries, perhaps millennia, harvesting grass seeds, digging roots, and cracking pinenuts. They had been derisively referred to as "Digger Indians" by influential observers, including champions of the downtrodden and dispossessed, such as Mark Twain (*Roughing It*).

So, Nan Smith collected a huge storehouse of lore, analyzed it in one volume, published much of the evidence in a second volume, and let a third batch lie fallow for decades. She learned little from the third batch that she did not already know and had not already demonstrated, to wit: the Great Basin is, indeed, a mythologic area. Basin societies speaking six mutually unintelligible languages and scattered from the Tehachapi Pass (Kawaiisu) in southern California to the edges of the Plains beyond the Rockies (Mowatavawatsiu Utes and Wind River Shoshone) share an array of lore that varies locally and by raconteur, and that is unmistakably simi-

lar. It is also unmistakably different from the lore of societies
to the east, north, west, and south.

Basin humor is ribald, spare, pointed, and often unspar-
ing. In her dissertation, an honest *magnum opus*, Nan reports that "trickster" tales comprise large proportions of the
myths told by most Basin raconteurs. As for stylistic features, she demonstrates that there is little repetition of num-
bers presumed to be sacred; frequent use of sexual and anal
references; and only modest salting with cultural detail.
Composite tales are made up of a combination of discrete
episodes. Novelistic tales where each episode depends on
the previous one are rare.

Ute tales, as the reader will soon learn, are almost always "concerned with the doings of animal-named characters
in a pre-human world" (Smith 1974:257). Interest centers in
action and plot, not motivation of action. If a moral or an explanation is offered ("And that's why dogs go around sniffing
assholes."), it is usually a just-so explanation tacked on at the
end of the tale. And the tale itself (no pun!) usually centers on
a single incident, yet locale is general, rather than specific.
Songs are not associated with dramatis personae.

Among the Utes, "the concept of a culture hero is not
important or elaborated" (ibid.). Coyote, or his brother,
Wolf, sometimes pop up as culture heroes, but Coyote is
more often the trickster and occasionally the hero from
whom "resultant gains to mankind from his adventures are
purely by-products" (ibid.). Hundreds of thousands of words
have been spilled over the meaning of the "trickster" in
American Indian myths.[15] And the trickster is a wonderful
character in many of the Ute myths.

For the past three decades, the close analysis of one or
two trickster tales have been sufficient to generate an article
in a professional journal for a modern "interpretive" anthropologist. Such was not the case during Nan's graduate student days. In the 1930s, a scholar might analyze a corpus of
lore, which included trickster myths, from some society, for
its cultural content, and then compare that content with the

stark reality of the hard, short, brutish life of the extractor, thereby providing cultural context as explanation of the purpose served by the myth. In most tale analyses, the authors themselves raised doubts about interpretation. Healthy skepticism about meaning was rather prominent, including investigations of the trickster.[16] Some, such as Katherine Spencer's fine piece on the Navajo origin myth or Melville Jacobs's articles and books on Clackamas Chinook oral traditions, are exemplary.[17]

But beginning around 1960 scholars, persuaded by Claude Lévi-Strauss, began pummeling North American myths, trickster stories in particular, seeking to reveal his (the trickster is almost always masculine) deep structure, providing a "deeper" explanation of the causes of the myth's structure than could be gained by dealing with such surface phenomena as cultural content.[18] Yet within twenty-five years, the structuralists became deconstructed by postmodern scholarship. The postmodernists have a way with words, such as "oxymoron," and the more strident practitioners among them claim that cultural content, and Freudian and structural explanations of tricksters, and everything else, are meaningless.[19]

Rather than plunge into the great debates between the schools of text analysts, I commend you to read "Eye Juggler" in the following pages (p. 5). "Eye Juggler" is different from my favorite Ute eye juggler story, but it will do.[20] In this version an observer uses a wish (formulaic magic) to cause a juggler to lose the objects he is juggling—his eyes. The juggler, a man, sniffs his way to his wives, nestles his head on one and rests his legs on the other and goes to sleep. Appalled at his eyeless sockets, the wives escape from him and run to a cliff. The eyeless juggler sniffs his way to them and plunges over the cliff. The women peer over the cliff and see that he is bruised, but still with the living. Indeed, they watch him eat his own leg, which had been severed in the fall. Undaunted, the husband reports to his wives at the top of the cliff that he is "eating the best deer meat you ever tasted."

In the 1930s, studies of folklore—myths, jests, märchen, epics, and the like—were unpublished for the most part.[21] Nan had to track down dozens of small collections languishing in the notebooks of observers. If published, the lore was relegated to the appendices of ethnographies about American Indian cultures. If the lore did not appear in appendices, and if the ethnographer collected a large batch of lore, it may have been published in *The Journal of American Folklore*. And if the collection was especially large and if the ethnographer wrote a few pages analyzing the cultural content of the lore, the collection may have appeared as a monograph in one of several ethnology or folklore series. These last were rare.

Nan produced a huge collection of lore and an analysis for it. Perhaps it was too large. No parts of it have made it to press until now. Here we are treated to a rich selection of the lore she collected among the Northern Utes in 1936 and 1937.

—JOSEPH G. JORGENSEN

Notes

1. Nan was known as Anne M. Cooke when she conducted her doctoral dissertation research among the Northern Ute. She married Eastburn Smith about the time she completed her doctoral dissertation in 1939, and thereafter was known as Nan Smith.

2. The Indian Claims Commission Act of 1946 established the Indian Claims Commission, a legal body comprising commissioners appointed by Presidential administrations charged with hearing and redressing grievances brought by Indian tribes against the federal government, especially on questions of broken and unratified treaties and other violations of dignity and property. Grievances, if justified by the evidence, were redressed with cash judgments. Legal arguments were conducted before the Commission by attorneys for Indian tribal plaintiffs who were pitted against defense attorneys for the United States. Evidence for both sides was prepared by anthropologists and ethnohistorians, such as the estimable Julian H. Steward, and Anne M. Cooke (Smith).

3. Similar to most federal legislation for Indians, the General Allotment Act (GAA) had a hoary history of implementation. Greed, ignorance, deceit, abuse, and sharp practices were its hallmarks on most reservations. If allottees refused allotments, the government often made allotments of the agents' choosing anyway. In theory, the GAA provided 40 acres of arable land to every living adult male on tribal rolls. Rules were followed loosely. On some reservations "satraps" (leaders appointed by the federal government) were given larger allotments than the average allottee. At Northern Ute, Uncompaghres were allotted land recognized by practice and by erstwhile Uinta Reservation boundaries as Uinta–White River land. In addition, Uncompaghre males over eighteen received 160 acres each, whereas Uinta and White River males were to receive 80 acres. Other living Utes, male and female, were to receive 40 acres. White Rivers, for the most part, refused allotments, and in 1907, following Saponose Cuch, fled the reservation, only to be returned under military escort in 1908 (see my *Sun Dance Religion* 1972:54–56). This occurred about the time of visits to the Northern Utes by Edward Sapir and J. Alden Mason. Neither of these scholars addressed the political and economic conditions of the Utes, nor did Kroeber a decade earlier when Utes hotly protested allotments. There were no provisions for future generations and no provisions for transfer of allotments at the death of the allottee. Heirs of the allottee became joint heirs of the allotment. In order to work the allotment land, heirs had to be in agreement. Thus, it was easier for the Bureau of Indian Affairs to lease the land to non-Indians than to adjudicate disputes among heirs.

4. Mormons, members of the Church of Jesus Christ of Latter-day Saints, acquired erstwhile Indian land by purchase (.65 to 1.25 per acre), or free through provisions of the Homestead, Desert Land Entries, Timber, Timber and Stone, or Mining Acts.

5. The Uinta Basin of eastern Utah stretches about 150 miles from the Strawberry River drainage on the west to the Green River on the east, and 50 miles from the Uinta Mountains on the north to the Tavaputs Plateau on the south.

6. A vicious feedback system ran most Utes hopelessly into debt: no water, no farm product; no farm product for sale, no cash for water. In 1946, with the intent of redressing some of their grievances, the Uinta and White River bands filed a suit in the U.S. Court of Claims for wrongful and wasteful use of tribal trust funds in the Uinta Irrigation Project. The grievance was not satisfied, in part because it takes an act of Congress to allow the government to be sued in the Court of Claims. Such bills were seldom enacted.

7. These disputes, including new ones, continue, although in 1954 the Northern Ute Tribe availed itself of termination provisions enabled by a "sense of Congress." Full-bloods and mixed-bloods legally dissociated and assumed proportional shares of the tribal estate (27 percent to the mixed-bloods). Mixed-bloods, by Ute definition, are persons with 50 percent Ute

blood or less. Full-bloods are persons with 50 percent Ute blood or more. Persons with 50 percent Ute blood could choose to enroll as a full-blood or a mixed-blood.

8. In 1933 the Northern Utes were awarded $1.2 million dollars (held in a 1 percent federal trust account) for one million acres appropriated from them for a national forest in 1905, pursuant to implementation of the General Allotment Act.

9. These issues are covered in some detail in chapter 5 (pages 146–73) of my *Sun Dance Religion: Power for the Powerless* (Chicago: University of Chicago Press, 1972).

10. Anne M. Smith, *Ethnography of the Northern Utes*, Papers in Anthropology, no. 17, Santa Fe: Museum of New Mexico Press, 1974. Herinafter referred to as Smith 1974.

11. I am reminded how rapidly technology changes. In the 1930s the original dissertation was submitted in typescript. Copies were produced on fine onionskin paper by carbon paper underlay. Nan's dissertation didn't even benefit from the consistent pressure afforded by an electric typewriter.

12. Northern Paiute, or Paviotso, language communities were scattered along the eastern slopes of the Sierra and the Cascades from Owens Valley in the south to Burns, Oregon in the north, fanning out as far east as the area near Fort Hall, Idaho (Bannock). The closest congeners of the Northern Paiute were the Western Mono of the Yosemite Park region on the west side of the Sierra divide. Shoshone speakers fanned out in a cone-shaped distribution from Panamint, south of Death Valley in California, to the Wind River Valley (Big Horn) in central Wyoming. Ute–Southern Paiute speakers, whose closest congeners were the Kawaiisu of the Tehachapi Pass region of southern California, fanned out along the south flank of the Great Basin along the north side of the Colorado River to about Denver on the eastern flank of the Rocky Mountains.

Many years after Nan established the Great Basin as a mythologic area, I began an analysis of about a hundred Basin ethnic groups pursuant to a much larger analysis of western American Indian languages, environments, and cultures at the time of first Contact (*Western Indians*, San Francisco: W. H. Freeman, 1980). My collaborator, Harold E. Driver, told me that those fifty units were going to be as similar as peas in a pod. He was right. The differences were minor, and they distinguished Shoshone from Paviotso from Ute–Southern Paiute. So we selected twenty-two units from among the three languages, including Panamint, Kawaiisu, and Western Mono, to represent the Uto-Aztecans of the Basin and their closest relatives.

13. In this volume, 102 of the tales from these research ventures are published. All originally appeared in Volume II of Nan's dissertation.

14. In her dissertation, Anne M. Smith published tales she collected from Shoshone and Paviotso raconteurs and compared them with earlier collections from Basin raconteurs. Upon completion of the dissertation Nan felt she had not collected enough tales from Shoshone and Paviotso

raconteurs to provide adequate comparisons with the Northern Ute tales. She sought advice from J. Alden Mason at the University of Pennsylvania Museum, and in 1939 again ventured into the Great Basin to collect tales, this time exclusively from Paviotso and Shoshone raconteurs. She compared her collection with those of other scholars, including unpublished notes by Edward Sapir on the Utes and Southern Paiutes, M. L. Zigmond on the Panamint Shoshone and the Kawaiisu (the latter most closely related to Southern Paiute), Beatrice Whiting on the Northern Paiute, and Edgar Elias Siskin on the Washo (a "Hokan"-speaking group near Lake Tahoe). Nan located other small, unpublished and published collections on the Chemehuevi (Southern Paiute), Wind River Shoshone, Northern Shoshone (Lemhi and Fort Hall), Gosiute (Western Shoshone), Western Shoshone, Owens Valley Paiute (Paviotso), and the Walapai (a Yuman-speaking group near the Grand Canyon). At this writing, a companion volume, *Shoshone Tales*, is in press (University of Utah Press, 1993).

15. Analyses of North American Indian trickster myths, complete with excellent bibliographies, are Mac L. Rickets, "The North American Indian Trickster," *History of Religions* 5 (1966): 327–50, and Guy R. Swanson, "Tricksters in Myths and Families: Studies of the Meaning and Sources of 'Pregenital' Relations," 259–308, in Leland H. Donald, ed., *Themes in Ethnology and Culture History. Essays in Honor of David F. Aberle*, Berkeley: Folklore Institute, 1987. Paul Radin's *The Trickster, A Study in American Indian Mythology*, New York: Philosophical Library, 1956, is a famous assessment of the trickster themes.

16. The trickster can be a culture hero saving all Indians in one myth, but stealing his food, cohabiting with his daughters, and sending gullible, innocent persons to their death in other myths. Perhaps, as Sky Masterson's daddy told him, never think you're are so smart that you aren't a mark. Especially don't count on something, even when you're sure you're right, because "someday someone is going to bet you $50 that a Jack of Spades in an unopened deck of cards will spit right in your eye, and as sure as you make the bet, that Jack will spit right in your eye." Life is not predictable. Indeed, it is harsh. The trickster reflects life.

17. Katherine Spencer, *Reflection of Social Life in the Navajo Origin Myth*, University of New Mexico Publications in Anthropology, no. 3, 1947; and Melville Jacobs, *The Content and Style of an Oral Literature: Clackamas Chinook Myths and Tales*, Viking Fund Publications in Anthropology, no. 26, 1959.

18. The eclipse of structuralism has led to less credible analyses of myths in which the argument goes something like this: if an ethnographer collects and interprets a myth, the interpretation is not an empirical analysis of the subject (the person who related the myth) nor an analysis of the story the subject told (the text). It is a statement about the ethnographer, the observer. But when that analysis is read by a critic, the critic is not reading the ethnographer's analysis, rather, s/he is imperfectly analyzing her/his self as self interprets the myth. Postmodernism (deconstruction) in anthropology is argued in George E. Marcus and Michael Fischer, 1986,

Anthropology as Cultural Critique: An Experimental Moment in the Human Sciences, Chicago: University of Chicago Press. A guide and roadmap to post-modernist cant, assumptions, and methods can be found in Pauline Marie Rosenau, 1992, *Post-Modernism and the Social Sciences*, Princeton: Princeton University Press. Claude Lévi-Strauss isn't mentioned in Rosenau's book.

19. These birds are saying something like, "You can't say that, but I can, or perhaps my language can, but don't take the language so seriously, because it is an artifact, after all. And anyway, what is the subject here?"

20. Many Indian societies in the American West had proficient jugglers. Among the Yuman speakers they tended to be women. Among the Ute the juggler is usually male, at least when the raconteur is female. In my favorite version, coyote sees a person juggling and decides to give it a go himself. He can't find any object near at hand, so he pops out his eyes and juggles them. They are lost soon after. Coyote, now blind, sniffs his way around.

21. The exception is, of course, Stith Thompson and several hundred European scholars. The analysis of folklore types is a time-honored tradition in Europe, from which Nan's study profited (a neat summary of the European tradition can be found in Stith Thompson's *The Folktale*, New York: Dryden, 1946). Spier was aware of Stith Thompson's classic distributional analysis of the Star Husband tale (Pleiadies myth) in which variants of tales of the same type told within and among various ethnic, social, and language groups are analyzed for similarities and differences. The object is to determine differences in form (structure) and variations and similarities in distributions before reconstructing the probable history of the tale and the uses to which it has been put.

Editor's Note

These Uinta and Uncompahgre tales were collected in Utah during the summer of 1937. The White River tales were collected in 1936 and 1937. The Uinta tale-tellers lived near White Rocks, the Uncompahgre tale-tellers lived between Fort Duchesne and Ouray, and the White River tale-tellers lived at White Rocks, Fort Duchesne, and Myton.

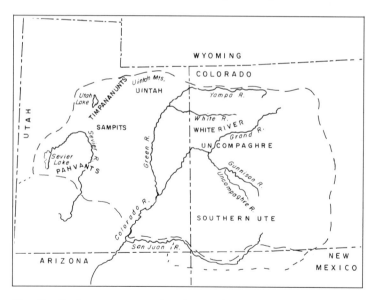

Ute distribution, pre-reservation times. (Courtesy of Museum of New Mexico Press.)

Uinta Tales

Uintas, White Rocks, 1909. Edward Sapir. Marriott Library Special Collections.

The Mock Hunter

Coyote went hunting. He had two wives. He killed two squirrels. The women were hungry and he came back and said, "I killed two great, big buffalo and they are way over there in the sagebrush. Tomorrow morning we will go get them." They went over next day and saw a great, big pile of sagebrush. "There it is," he said and he took those women over there. They began to take the sagebrush off and took it off and took it off, and when it was all off there were just the little squirrels.

The women used to be big and fat, but after they were Coyote's wives they just got poor and were starving to death. The brother of one of these women went over there because he heard his sister was starving, and he got her and brought her home. Then after that, when Coyote used to say, "I killed a certain animal," nobody believed him. They just laughed at him.

—STELLA KURUMP

The Council of the Bears

There were people who went hunting. They found a place where a rock was just round, bowl-shaped. They heard somebody talking. They couldn't see anyone, and they said, "Who is talking?" One man went and looked in that place and he thought he heard someone talking. He peeked in and saw lots of bears. Then they tied their horses in a certain place. One man was standing on the edge of this rock basin where the bears were and he motioned to the others to come and look in there. The bears were talking to each other.

One bear asked another, "What's your name and where do you come from?" And the bear answered and said, "I come from Bear Ear." He asked the other, "Where are you from?" and he answered, "I am from Sagebrush Hill and I told my little ones to be sure and make a fire when I am coming so when I get home there will be a fire." He asked another bear, "Where do you come from?" and he said, "I came from a Tall Hill and I asked my kids to make a fire when I am coming home." He asked another bear the same question and he said he came from Red Hill.

Then the bears were talking to each other and asked each other what they did. One said, "Oh, I often kill a hunter." Another said, "I killed a woman who was picking serviceberries." One bear said, "There was a bunch of squaws digging roots and I killed one of them. I took after her and threw her down and tore her to pieces."

After they got through talking they started smoking. At the head of the row was a big bear with a big pipe. They passed the pipe around. Before he passed the pipe, he said to the next bear, "How do they pass the pipe to you, you old Sloppy Foot?" "How do they pass it to you?" he said to the next one, calling him by name—Willow Earrings. Then he asked the next bear, "How do they hold it to give you a smoke?" "Oh, hand it to me with your two hands." Then the very last bear got up and spoke and said, "Yes, we all met here in this place. Be on the lookout or our flesh will be eaten by some hunters. We will be in danger soon." And he started crying.

Then they all started to dance and all talk the same way, afraid that they would be eaten by hunters. Then the last bear spoke up and said, "Our flesh would be game for the hunters." And the hunters who were watching shot at this bear. And the bears did not know from what direction the arrows were coming, and they started milling around and fighting and they all got killed. The hunters left the bears on top of each other on the rock. They were scared because they never heard bears talk before.

—Agnes Maianna

Eye Juggler

Once there was a bunch of people. They were going along, playing and talking, and taking out their eyes. They were laughing and having a good time. Someone saw them and said, "I wish they would never get their eyes back." This man said (to himself), "I wish, in the medicine way, one of them would lose his eyes."

The man who lost his eyes had two wives. He smelled his way out to his wives. They were both sitting down. Then he came and lay between them and put his head on one and his legs on the other. The women saw his eyes were kind of wrong. He had tied a bandage over his eyes. He fell asleep when he was lying down and they wondered what had happened to him and they pulled that bandage. Then they saw what had happened and they didn't like him. While he was asleep they laid his feet and head on the ground and they ran away. They ran to where there was a big rock, a cliff. Then one said, "If he follows us he will fall right in there. He will smell his way to where we went."

Then he woke up. He felt that his wives were gone, and he followed their smell and went to the edge of the cliff. They hid back there and he fell off down the cliff. After he fell, the women saw him. He broke one of his legs clear off and he was eating the marrow from it. He heard them laughing. Then he said, "Where are you? I am down here. I am eating the best deer you ever tasted." Then they ran off.

—Agnes Maianna

Ghost Robs Dove

There was a young fellow who went hunting. He was Dove's son. While he was on his way, Ghost came and led him off. When Ghost took him, he used to go hunting every day and bring back his game to Ghost. So, when Mother Dove used to fly nearby, Ghost would say, "Don't listen to that bird. Don't let her take you away." One day while he was out hunting, he met his mother and she said, "Son, next time you go hunting, you take whatever you kill and put it high up on the cliff." So he did and he told Ghost where he put the meat. So the she-ghost tied her pubic hair together and made a long, stiff rod to use to pull down that game. Then she said, when she couldn't get it down, "There must have been somebody who talked to that boy." Then the boy and his mother ran away and left the she-ghost trying to get the meat.

When the mother and son were running away, they were so tired that when they met a bull snake they asked him if they could hide in his hole. He said yes, and they crawled into his hole. Ghost came after them. Then the snake said, "I have something here that will kill Ghost. I'll set fire to this pitch and hit Ghost with it. As soon as I set this afire, you two doves go." So he did that and away they went again. Ghost just kicked around in that pitch. She was all stuck up and tried so hard to get out of it. If that snake hadn't killed Ghost, we would all be bothered with ghosts today.

—STELLA KURUMP

Porcupine Tricks Coyote

There was a big river, and Porcupine was on one side and the buffalo were on the other. Porcupine said, "Come and get me and carry me across the river," and one came across, the best one. "How will I take you? In my nose?" "No, you might

Uintas, White Rocks, 1909. Edward Sapir. Marriott Library Special Collections.

snot on the way and blow me out." "Where are you going to ride then, in my anus?" "No, you might defecate and push me out." Well, will you ride on my back?" "No, you might bump me off." "Maybe you can get between my toes?" "No, I might fall off." "Will you ride in my ear?" Porcupine said, "No, I want to get inside of you." So he got inside through the rectum. He could tell by the sound of the hoofs when Buffalo had reached the edge of the river, and Porcupine whipped around his spines into the heart and lungs and killed Buffalo.

Then he wondered what he would butcher with and hollered around. Coyote came along and heard him. "What did you say? I heard you saying something; you wanted something to butcher with." "Oh, no. I was saying something else." Finally Porcupine admitted he wanted something to butcher with. So Coyote said, "Whoever can jump the farthest over Buffalo will get to butcher him. Coyote jumped over, but Porcupine landed right on Buffalo. Coyote butchered him while Porcupine watched. Coyote took the best parts of the animal and told Porcupine he could have the worst guts. He told Porcupine to take the entrails and feed the water-skaters with them. Porcupine ate the entrails and gave the bugs what he was supposed to eat himself.

So Coyote said, "Did you feed my bugs what I told you to?" "Yes." "Well, I am going to ask them myself if you fed them what I told you to feed them." The bugs said, "He fed us the worst part and he ate the best part." So Coyote was mad and beat up Porcupine, and Porcupine died. After a while he came to again. So Coyote beat him up again and mashed his head all up. Then Coyote sat down and defecated right by him. Then his feces hollered, "Porcupine is moving again!" so Coyote gave him another beating. Coyote started off again and the feces kept talking and Coyote got mad at it and hit it with his tail and then went on. When he went, Porcupine got up and went over to the meat and got on top and said, "I want the pines to grow." The pines began to grow and Porcupine took the meat and went up on top of the pines.

Coyote came back after a while and brought all his family, his wives and children. Stick-Hanging-on-His-Hip was his youngest child. He went on ahead to where the meat was. He said, "The girls were all glad I killed that Porcupine." They were going to make him porcupine-quill moccasins. Coyote couldn't find where he left the meat. He said, "There is all this timber here." There were just a few quills where he had been beating up Porcupine.

The little fellow looked up and saw Porcupine up in the tree. Porcupine said, "All of you lie down under the tree and I'll throw down some meat." So they all laid on their backs and had their eyes shut. Then Porcupine took the neck of the buffalo and said, "I wish that littlest fellow would move so he won't get hurt, and then he threw that meat and the little fellow moved and all Coyote's family were killed except him.

Porcupine told the little fellow to climb the tree, and he

did, and Porcupine fed him so much meat. And he got so full he wanted to defecate. Porcupine told him to go to the end of the limb, and when he sat down, Porcupine shook that limb and the little fellow fell down and when he hit the ground, he burst. Porcupine said, "That's the way it's going to be. You are Stick- Hanging-on-His-Hip now but people are going to call you ᵧᵘwo'lwic after this."

So Porcupine got down and took his meat home with him, and when he got home there were strange children there. His wife had married Coyote. Coyote had beat him to his wife. Then he got mad and Coyote said, "My friend, there have been a lot of fellows here, seeing your wife. That's why I came, so they would leave her alone." But Porcupine was mad anyway and said he was going to kill him. Coyote lit out and ran and Porcupine shot at him. Porcupine killed all of Coyote's children. Then he went back home and lived.

—STELLA KURUMP

The Man Who Visited Bear

There was once a man. He was going to see his aunt. It was in winter time. His aunt was Bear. He went up there and saw his aunt at the door, standing on her hind legs. Bear didn't like this man coming to see her, that is why she reared up. Bear killed the man. There was another fellow who wanted to go see Bear. After Bear ate the first man, she came out for air and stretched out and the second man saw her. He stood right in front of Bear. Bear liked the man. "Hello, Aunt. What are you doing?" Then he told Bear, "I came to see you, my aunt. I'm going to stay with you this winter."

So he went in and lay down. He stayed there all the time. They used to get up early in the morning. She used to dig around where she stored the berries and give the man a handful. Then it came spring. Bear said, "I guess it's time for you to leave. I am going to have my little ones." "I'll come see you again after you have them." Bear had two little cubs and then the man came to see them. "All right, you can go home, the snow is all gone now." He smelled different when he came back from Bear. He smelled sour.

—AGNES MAIANNA

Water Boy

John Duncan says he has heard a story from the Gosiute Indians about Water Boy. A baby was in a cradleboard leaned against a tree while its mother picked berries. The baby turned into a Water Boy and disappeared. Water Boy swallows people. They used to be afraid of them.

—JOHN DUNCAN
(Lincoln Picket, translator)

Water Boy Wrestles with Tiger

There was a Water Boy (*ba aputs*) once. There was some ice that went straight up into the air. Ba Aputs used to challenge people to come and wrestle with him, and he would throw them against the ice and break their backs. Bear went and wrestled with him. He stayed with Ba Aputs a while but he couldn't lick him. Bear got killed. Then Lion tackled him. He gave him a hard wrestle, but Ba Aputs licked him too.

Then Tiger fought next. Some of that ice stuck with the points toward them and when Ba Aputs tackled Tiger, Tiger had wrapped his tail around one of the icicles so that Ba Aputs couldn't throw him down. Tiger threw Ba Aputs into the icicles. Then Ba Aputs got hold of Tiger again, but Tiger threw Ba Aputs down again. Ba Aputs got real mad and he was real powerful and Tiger just then got all in and got so heavy. Every time Ba Aputs tried to pull him up he would

John Duncan's camp, 1909. Edward Sapir. Marriott Library Special Collections.

stretch. Then Tiger got over that feeling and got mad. When Tiger got mad he made those icicles sharper so they were like pins on the end. Ba Aputs got mad and all the icicles melted and formed just like a wall and then Ba Aputs went toward Tiger again.

When they wrestled again, the ice where Ba Aputs was going to throw him got sharp again but Tiger just stepped over the points and wrapped his tail around one and threw old Ba Aputs and killed him. So Tiger said, "Now that I've killed you, you're only going to be a *ba aputs*, and you will only scare children from now on." Soon after, they heard old Ba Aputs crying down in the creek.

—STELLA VICTOR

Siants

A man had gone hunting, leaving his wife and baby in the tent. While he was away Siants came. The woman was frightened by him; he had his feet and fingers cut off. The woman knew the direction her husband had taken when he went hunting and she followed him. He had made a fire and when the woman found him she said, "Siants came and scared me and I left the baby."

When morning came they went back to the tent. When they got near they could hear the baby crying. Siants was lying there with the baby. He had the baby down between his legs and was nursing the baby. The baby's mouth was foaming. The father rushed in and pulled that baby out and beat the Siants. The baby had been sucking Siants' penis. The father pressed the baby's stomach, which was all puffed out. He tried to press out all the stuff the baby had sucked in. The baby recovered and they killed Siants.

—Kurump Longhair
(Stella LaRose, translator)

The Rescue of the Captured Child

Long ago there lived some people who used to battle with other people. They would go from a place in the mountains down into the valley. They camped in a narrow place and the enemy sneaked up on them. One of them saw the enemy coming and some of the people were able to escape, warned by the barking dogs. The enemy rushed the camp and captured a little boy. They took him away with them. Some of the people wanted to go search for the child, and the child's mother wanted to go with them. But the men were afraid to go. One middle-aged man named Kanitovic liked the sister of the boy who had been captured. He offered to try and find the boy and the family told him he could have the daughter for his wife if he brought back the stolen child.

Kanitovic trailed the enemy. He was gone a long time. He went up on the mountains in the daytime and looked around. When he was sitting there he saw a man on horseback going along a trail. Kanitovic sneaked up on that man and got close to him. He shot at him and killed him with his bow and arrow. Then he dragged him into the bushes, removed all his clothes, and put them on himself. Then he mounted the slain man's horse and continued trailing the enemy. When he got to the river he saw fresh tracks. He thought he had better go up on a hill and see what he could see.

He saw from the hill that the enemy had made camp. He could see their tents. He was close enough so they could hear him and he called like a coyote. They heard him and he started down from the mountain. He rode on down to camp. The man Kanitovic had killed was married. When the people saw his clothes and his horse, they thought it was the man Kanitovic had killed. Kanitovic could just talk in signs to them. Kanitovic told them he had gone through the desert where there was no water, and his tongue had swelled so that he could not talk.

They had the little captured boy tied way up in the fork of a tree, and with him was a bunch of Sun Dance weed. Next day they went on building the corral, a bunch of forked poles around the tree in which the boy was tied. This was a Sun Dance corral.

The boy stayed in the tree four nights. Kanitovic could not figure out how to get the boy. When he had told the people about his hard luck in the desert, they had made him chief. One night Kanitovic told all the people to rest, to sleep good, and he got up in the night. All the people were inside the corral and he told them to sleep well. He stayed at the entrance and said that he would watch the boy. Toward morning they all began to doze off and sleep. The little boy was tied so that he could not move. His hands and feet were tied. One man sat next to the big tree in the center. He fell asleep. Kanitovic crawled up to him and hit him with a rock.

The noise roused the other men, but Kanitovic lay down and pretended to be asleep. Everything quieted down and Kanitovic got up and looked at the tree. He tried to figure out how he would get up there.

He had a rawhide rope. He threw one end up over the crotch, and then he pulled himself up the tree with this. He reached the little boy and asked him how he was. The little boy said, "I'm all right yet." Kanitovic untied the little boy and put him on his back. He fixed the brush the boy was sleeping in. Then he slid down the tree with the boy on his back. He walked over the man whom he had knocked out. There was another man right at the entrance of the corral who was sound asleep. Kanitovic thought he had better jump over this man, but he jumped right on his head and woke him up.

Kanitovic ran to the tent where his wife was (the wife of the man Kanitovic had killed) and told her that someone had stepped on his head and awakened him. The people hunted around and discovered that the boy was missing. Kanitovic hid the boy under a rawhide bag in his tent and lay down with his wife. He pretended to be asleep when the people came. He was snoring. They tried to wake him up, but he just groaned and pretended to be sound asleep and then he scolded them. He said, "Go back and watch. What are you doing out here?" They said, "He has escaped, he stepped on one man's head." So Kanitovic got up and said, "Well, we will have to look for him. Get your horses and start riding." They hunted all around while Kanitovic stayed at the camp. He told them he would keep watch there. They asked him, "How do you feel now? Is your tongue any better?" He used to eat nothing but soup because he said his tongue was so sore.

It was day then. Night came and Kanitovic said, "Tomorrow we will journey back to where we got that boy and look for him. Tonight we will have a big dance, a Turkey Dance." They made a big fire and all gathered around it. Kanitovic said, "I am going to leave for a few minutes. There is something I want to get at home." "All right," they said, but two fellows followed along behind him. He heard their footsteps so he just went into the tent and got his pipe and went back to where they were dancing. He must have gotten some kind of stuff he had to make them drowsy. He asked them to join him in smoking, and they all gathered around and passed his pipe around. Then they began to dance again, but they all got dizzy. "Well, I guess I will go put my pipe back again," he said. The fellows did not follow him this time.

When he got to camp he peeked out to see if anyone were watching. He could not see anyone, so he put that boy into the rawhide bag. His wife happened to come in when he was tying the bag. When he put it on his back, his wife began to call out. The people all came. He could not run fast and they caught him. The sun was coming up. He still had that boy tied to his back. They told him they would give him a big feast and then kill him. They said they would give him a lot of smokes and they got a lot of buffalo heads.

When Kanitovic used to dream, he dreamed that when he had enough tobacco smoke in him there would be smoke on the mountains. He made a little hole in the ground underneath his anus and that is where the smoke went. It went up to the mountains so it did not affect him. When they gave him all that meat to eat, he gave some to the boy. Kanitovic used to dream that when he got too much to eat, the rocks in the mountains would move around and make a noise. So he made another hole in the ground where that food was supposed to go and he thought about that dream and he did not get too full.

Then they lined up the buffalo heads a step's length apart, for him to step on. They guarded the poor fellow and told him to go down to the other end of the line. There were men on horseback on both sides of the line of heads and at the other end. If he missed one of those buffalo heads in stepping, he would have to do battle with them. So he balanced the little boy on his back. He ran on those heads. Just before he got to the last one he stumbled, and they all ran after him.

He ran and they shot at him. The men on horseback

reached him and he ran under the horses and they could not find him. He got away and then they saw him, and chased him, and he made for the horses to hide again. He would grab a horseman once in a while and throw him off. The horses got scared. When a man caught up with him, he would get under his horse and reach up and pull the rider off. The men had no more arrows left. When Kanitovic got under the horses he would tie his rope through the horse's bridle, then he would run under another horse and run his rope through his bridle until he got most of the horses tied up. The horses all ran into each other and got all tangled up and Kanitovic got ahead of the horses.

Kanitovic was all tired out. He went to a big tree. He still had his bow and arrows. He sat behind the tree and waited for his pursuers. They got their horses straightened out and ran after him. He sat there and shot at them with his bow and arrows. He killed them all except one and let him go back home to tell the news.

Kanitovic and the boy each took a horse and set out for home. He still had some arrows, and he shot rabbits for them to eat. They got near home and Kanitovic went up on a mountain to see just where they were. Kanitovic had stripped the men he killed and scalped them. Now he put some of the enemy's hair on an arrow and shot the arrow down home to where somebody could pick it up. One of the men picked it up, and the boy's father identified the arrow, for he had made it for his boy. So they started up the mountain to search. Kanitovic had made a fire up on the mountain. They all rushed to the fire and were glad. The girl Kanitovic wanted to marry went along too. Kanitovic and the boy were eating when the people arrived. They took the little boy. The boy's mother had formerly been mean about her daughter. Now she grabbed her little boy, then grabbed Kanitovic and dragged him over to her daughter. So they all went back to camp.

One night after that the enemy arrived again and attacked them. Kanitovic just stayed in his tent and told his

wife to get some supper for them. She was scared, but
Kanitovic wasn't. He ate and then he went and got his horse.
He killed an elk on his way to get his horse. They were still
fighting, but Kanitovic chased the chief of the enemy and
killed him. When the chief was killed, the others stopped
fighting and ran. The rest of the people scalped all the dead
enemies and took all their clothes. They danced that night.
They had won that battle.

—VICTOR

(Stella LaRose, translator)

Corn Lover

There was a young woman married to an old man. She used
to pretend to go after wood, but she would go among those
plants that grow like corn. She would break one of the ears
off. Her husband wondered what she did and one time he
watched her. She got one of those cobs, like corncobs, and
she masturbated with it.

Next day he took one of those things just his size and
fixed it on the ground. She saw it and sat on it and jumped up
and down on it and it killed her.

—NANAN

(Stella LaRose, translator)

Uncompahgre Tales

(Stella LaRose, translator)

Ute women and baby, 1936. Alden Hayes.

Coyote's Adventures

Coyote was going along the river. There were some Sage Hen children in front of him. He thought, "I'll urinate on them." So he did. The mother of the birds returned. "What is the matter with your eyes? What have you been doing?" They said, "Coyote was here and he urinated on us." "Which way did he go?" "He went down along the bank of the creek."

Sage Hen went behind and saw him traveling along. She flew around in front of him and hid. When he got close to her, she flew up suddenly and frightened him. He fell into the water and got his white leggings all wet. He crawled out on the other side of the creek. He took off his leggings and blanket and hung them up to dry.

He was lying by the river, looking in the water. He saw below him some chokecherries, big ones. He fished for them and grabbed, but all he got was sand. He tried again, but again got nothing but sand. He looked again, saw the berries, fished for them and brought up sand. He did it time and time again until he was exhausted. Then he got so tired he crawled under a bush and closed his eyes. After a while he turned over on his back and opened his eyes. When he looked up, there were the berries directly overhead.

He gathered lots of them. Then he went on his way and took the berries with him. He came to the place where Bear was. "Oh," said Bear, "my brother, where did you get your berries?" He said, "I got them far away, over on that mountain." Then he said, "No, I did not mean that. I got them not far from here." Bear said, "Let me go over there and get some berries. I will go down there and you can stay here with your nephews."

She went off and left him with her baby bear. Coyote thought, "I wonder what I can do with the boy." He cut the child's throat. The baby was in a cradleboard. Coyote laced a stick in the board so that it looked like a baby, and then he put the bear's head in the hood.

Mother Bear came back and said, "Did your nephew cry while I was gone?" "No, he didn't cry." Coyote had cooked the baby bear. He had boiled it. Bear said, "What are you cooking?" "Oh, some deer ran past here and I caught one of them. That is what I am cooking." Bear said, "I am glad, I will have a good meal." Coyote took some short willows and put the meat on them. Bear ate and ate. When all the meat was gone, Coyote left. When he got some distance from camp, he shouted back, "You have eaten your baby." "Was that my baby?" cried Bear. She chased him. She was angry.

She was getting near him when he crawled into a hole. She started digging at the hole trying to get at Coyote, but there was another opening to the tunnel and he got out that. He went to the cedars and got some pine gum and glued his eye on one side and pretended to be a cripple. He came to the spot where Bear was digging and said, "What are you doing?" Bear said, "The animal that killed my son went into this hole, that is why I am digging here." "Well," he said, "you will never get him became the animal that lives here has a long tunnel that goes out at the top of the mountains far away. I will prove it to you." He got some sagebrush and burned it at the entrance. There was a cloud on the tip of the mountain at that time and he said, "Look, see that smoke on top of the mountain?" It was just a cloud, but Bear believed him when he said it was the smoke. Coyote went limping away, and when he was some distance off, he shouted back, "You are Bear, who ate your little son." Bear said, "I knew it was that same person." She chased him.

Coyote crawled into another hole and out the exit on the

other side. This time he had a cane. He came back to where
Bear was digging and said, "What are you doing?" Bear said,
"I am digging for Coyote." "The animal that lives here has
too long a tunnel. You will never get him." This time he circled around her and shouted, "You ate your little one." When
she turned her head, he hit her with his *pogamoggan* and
killed her.

—Charlie Wash

Rabbit Tames Wood and Water

A long time ago there was a dove who had two little ones.
She lived under a rock. The mother dove went and gathered
seeds and was storing them away. While she was covering
the seeds with a rock, it fell on her and killed her. The two
little ones knew where their mother buried the food. They
made a hole and dug the seeds out with sticks. Their faces
were all scabby. They were untidy-looking youngsters. Their
faces were sore and bruised. Everything was mean to them.
The rocks would jump up and hit them. If they went to break
off a stick it would hit them. When they went for water, the
water would chase them.

Rabbit came to their camp and asked where their mother
was. "The rock killed her as she was storing some food for
us. It rolled on her." Rabbit said, "Why are you covered with
scabs and sores?" Rabbit wanted them to make a fire. They
told Rabbit how everything was hostile to them and hit them.
Rabbit said, "Go make a fire." They went after sticks, and
the sticks hit the children. Rabbit took his *pogamoggan* and
hit the sticks and said, "You are not going to be mean any
more. You are no longer going to fly at people." They made a
fire. Then Rabbit told them to go get water. Rabbit saw the
water rush at the dove children. He hit the water and said,
"You are going to be only water. People will drink you while
you are still."

Rabbit told the children to take him to the spot where

they had last seen their mother. Everything on the hill was hostile and frightened the children, but they stayed close to Rabbit. When they got to the spot, Rabbit pushed the rock off the mother. She woke up and rubbed her eyes and said, "I have been asleep." Rabbit said to the rock, when he pushed it away, "You are not going to be mean any more. You will not move around. You will stay in one place."

—Lulu Chepoose

Toad and Frog

Horned Toad had some children. Frog went to visit them. He said, "You are going to drown. The water will take you." So Toad started to think and thought, "We better move." They moved to a high place on the hill. It started to rain, and it rained and rained. The water came up high. There was a pond on the hill. Frog was sitting on the bank. The little toads told Frog, "When the water goes away, you are going to dry up and your feet will stick up in the air."

Toad went away. She came back sometime later to this place and there lay Frog, just as they told him he would. She went to him and spit on his chest. That refreshed him. He opened his eyes and said, "I have been asleep." That is how he came back to life.

—Ruth Nanants

Frog and Coyote Race

There was Coyote. He challenged Frog to run a race with him. "All right," he said, "we will run tomorrow, in the morning." That gave Frog a chance to gather the rest of the frogs and station them in different places. Frog and Coyote met in the morning. They counted, "One, two, three," and then

Uncompahgre man, Ouray, 1909. Edward Sapir. Marriott Library Special Collections.

they started. Frog jumped, but then another frog jumped on from where the first landed, like a relay race. Frog beat Coyote.

—RUTH NANANTS

Ghost Robs Dove

There was a dove who had two children. The mother used to go out gathering seeds and leave the babies at home. One baby was a girl, the other a boy. Then Echo came to them. The babies used to perch on the cedar. Echo asked what the one was and what the other was. Echo asked a second time, but the mother Dove had told the children never to answer.

Echo came and grabbed one of the children. She did not know whether it was the boy until she searched and found its penis. "Oh, is this why they never told me what it was?" Echo took the little boy. After a while he was grown up. All the time the mother wept and cried and longed for her son.

The boy, now grown up, met his mother when he flew around, but he did not know her. She had her eyes closed. Then he looked at her again. He looked at her feet and then at his own and he said, "She has shoes just like mine. She looks just like me." He took an arrow point and stuck it in her eyes and woke her up. She said, "Oh, my little boy that was lost. I am glad to see you." She asked him what game he killed. "Do you kill buffalo and deer? Do you kill big animals to eat?" He told her he did. Then his mother said, "The next time you kill a buffalo, butcher it, pack it in the skin, and put it high up in that cedar for Echo." He did this. Echo wanted the boy for a husband.

She tried to get the meat, but it was so high that she could not reach it. She said, "I wonder why he put it so high." She took one of her pubic hairs to reach the meat with, but that was not long enough, so she joined another pubic hair to the first, and using them as a rod, pushed the meat down. When she got the meat on the ground, she picked it up and put it on her back. The skin broke and the meat spilled out. She fixed it, tied new knots, and put the pack on her back again. It broke once more. She tried again to tie it up. She said, "My husband could escape during this time." She would walk a short distance and the pack would break again and she would have to stop and fix the pack.

Meantime, Dove Mother had joined her boy. She asked the boy where he slept and he told her. They put a stump in his bed and covered it up. Echo finally arrived home with the meat. She cried, "Why are you still in bed?" She ran and sat on that stump in his bed and jumped up and down on it. She thought it was her husband. Then she uncovered it and saw it was just a stick. Then she set out in pursuit of her husband. Mother Dove and her son were running. Dove said, "We will go to your grandfather's place." It was up on the cliff. They looked back and saw Echo following them. "We better hurry, she is coming rapidly."

The grandfather was Rattlesnake. He was sitting in his door, grinding something. When they got there Dove told him how Echo had stolen her son and how she had just gotten him back. "She is pursuing us and she is not far behind. We just got here in time." Snake wrapped the birds up in the grinding stone and threw them out. Then he crawled back into his cave and let his penis stick up. When Echo got there and saw it, she jumped up and down on it. While she was having intercourse, the cave kept getting smaller and smaller. Finally there was only a small entrance left, just large enough for Snake to get out. He went out and Echo was left shut up in the cave. She never got out. That is how Echo got in the cliffs.

—Lulu Chepoose

Coyote Learns to Fly

Coyote heard the geese cry as they flew over him. He said, "Let me be your leader." They landed on the ground near him and each bird gave him a few feathers. They said, "Don't make any noise before the rest of us do." Coyote was practicing flying and how to make the same cry that the geese gave. When they were ready to take off, he was ready to fly with them.

They flew over some camps, and every time they got near a camp, Coyote was the first one to cry, even though they had told him not to. When they flew to a spring, Coyote would fly down first, and every time he took a drink, he would urinate in the spring. The geese would come after him and they would drink the water in which Coyote had urinated. When they flew over camps, Coyote always called out first. The geese said, "He is going to get us in trouble one of these days. Next time we fly over a camp we will pull all the feathers out of him." They flew off and then all at once they removed their feathers from Coyote. Coyote could no longer fly. He cried because he could fly no more.

—LULU CHEPOOSE

Coyote Breaks a Bird's Leg

Coyote was sitting, watching Bear. He wanted to kill her. He was sneaking around. A little bird was there and saw him. The bird kept saying, "Coyote is moving, Coyote is moving." When he said that, Coyote got angry and threw a rock at him and broke his leg. Then Coyote was sorry and said, "Oh, I broke my friend's leg." He got some grass and tied it around the leg and fixed it. Then he killed Bear and took the claws. He made a necklace of them for the bird. That is why the bird has black around his neck.

—RUTH NANANTS

Coyote Mistakes Louse for Buffalo

There was Coyote. He had lice. He was going along in the brush, looking about. He saw a big buffalo and stole up on him. When he got to the place where he thought he had seen the buffalo, there was nothing there. When he returned to the first spot, he looked up and saw the buffalo in the same place. He stole up on him again, but when he got there, there was no buffalo. He returned and when he looked up again, there was the buffalo. Then he got tired. He discovered it was one of his own lice, hanging in his eyelashes, which looked like a buffalo when he looked up. When he discovered it was a louse, he took it off and stamped on it.

—CHARLIE WASH

Charlie Wash's family, White Rocks, 1909. Left: Stella; right: Mary. Edward Sapir. Marriott Library Special Collections.

The Lost Sisters

A man lived with his two sisters. The man went away and he lost track of his sisters. Mountain Lion, Hawk, and Fly met the man. He asked if they knew anything about his sisters. "They live far away." Lion gave him some of the hair from his armpit and said he was giving him some of his strength. "When anyone attacks you, say 'Mountain Lion,' and I will be with you. You will have my strength." Fly gave him one pair of his wings and said he would have wings. Hawk gave him feathers from his wings and said, "Now you will be able to fly. You are all outfitted now. Go on your journey." Eagle also gave him some strength.

When the man started, he shouted, "Hawk!" and then he

Small canvas tepee and brush shelter, Charlie Wash's camp, 1909.
Edward Sapir. Marriott Library Special Collections.

flew. Then he walked for a time. While he was walking he
saw an enemy and he shouted, "Fly!" He was very near the
enemy, but he turned into a fly and flew around the horses of
the enemy and escaped. He left those enemies wondering
where he had vanished. After he left them, he said, "Hawk!"
and then he flew. He flew until he came to some tents. There
was a woman there and he asked if she knew anything about
his sisters. He was searching for his sisters. He spoke of
them by name and the woman said, "I am your sister." She
said her husband was a very dangerous man, a killer. "You
better hide in the rocks there, I am afraid he might kill you
when he comes. When he gets near home it will begin to
sprinkle a little rain."

When the husband was near home it rained a little. When
the husband came, the man saw that he was a hawk. "I won-

der," he said, "How they live as husband and wife. I wonder
how she lives with him." He went to the tent and could see
feathers there, but Hawk had changed into a handsome man.
Hawk said, "I can smell something strange. There has been
someone here today." His wife said, "It was my younger
brother, your brother-in-law." Hawk said, "Where is he? Go
get him." She found her brother and brought him home. He
stayed there all night. Then he asked where the other sister
was. "She lives far away, by the lake. You will see a woman
there and it will be your sister." Her husband, Hawk, gave
the man one of his feathers and strength to fly.

When he left, he shouted, "Hawk!" and away he flew.
He went to the camp by the lake. He said to the woman
there, "Are you my sister who left home long ago?" The
woman said, "Yes, I am she." She said her husband was a
very dangerous man. "You better go away from here and
wait over there until he comes." He wondered what kind of
man she was married to.

While he was waiting, he saw the water begin to move
and a big fish emerge. Fish went to his wife and said, "It
smells strange here. Someone has been here." She said,
"Yes, my younger brother was here." Fish said, "Go get
your brother. Bring him here." The man was wondering how
Fish could sleep with his sister. But when he looked again, he
saw a fish skin lying there and Fish was a fine-looking man.
Fish gave him one of his fins so he would be a strong swim-
mer. Then he crawled into the fish skin and turned into a fish.

The woman said, "Way over across the lake lives a
moose who has drowned many people. Perhaps if he sees
you he will drown you." Her brother saw a big, tall man. That
man was Moose and he tackled our hero. Then the man said,
"Why, he is not strong." All the men who had been drowned
by Moose were under the water. Moose told these men, "I
saw a man. I don't know where he came from. He is a
stranger." While the man and the Moose were struggling,
the man called, "Lion!" and he had the strength of the mountain lion and conquered Moose Man. Moose said, "If anyone

ever kills me, the water will dry up or else it will overflow."
Lion's strength succeeded in killing Moose. The man
watched, and when the soul of Moose left the body, he
chased it. He saw a fish. He dived and caught up with
Moose's soul. The soul went to the place where Moose had
been accustomed to stay in the water and Fish Man got it
there. Then he rescued those people that Moose had
drowned.

—Charlie Wash

Tarbaby

Coyote and Rabbit planted a garden. Then they irrigated.
Coyote told Rabbit to stay home while he went hunting. He
wanted to get out and rustle around. "You stay here." The
watermelons were half-ripe at this time. Coyote went away.
After he had gone, Rabbit went to the garden. He found the
big melons gone. Rabbit wondered what had happened to the
melons. He got some pine gum and put it around the melons.
He told the gum, "Be sure and hold the thief fast."

Night came and Rabbit went to bed. Early in the morning
he went to the melon patch. He heard someone saying, "Let
go of me. I'll hurt you if you don't let go." Rabbit took a stick
and went down and whipped the animal that was caught in the
gum. He discovered that the thief was Coyote.

—Achis

Coyote and Skunk

Skunk was out on the flats. There were many prairie dogs
there that he had killed with his smell. He gathered them and
made a big fire. When there were hot ashes, he laid the prairie dogs in them side by side. Coyote came by and challenged
him to a race. Coyote said, "Whoever wins shall eat the prai-

Ute children, 1936. Alden Hayes.

rie dogs." Skunk agreed. Coyote took the lead. Skunk kept up with him for a little while and then Coyote got ahead. Skunk turned around and came back to the place where the prairie dogs were cooking. He picked out the biggest and fattest prairie dogs and put them in a hole before Coyote got back. The hole was quite a way off. Skunk sat there and waited.

When Coyote got back he was all out of breath. He said, "My friend is still running. I bet he will feel like eating when he gets here." Coyote walked around. When he came near the fire he reached down and picked up a little prairie dog by the tail. He picked up another and saw that it, too, was a little one. There were nothing but little ones left for him. Then he set out to track Skunk, and he saw where Skunk had taken the fat dogs. He looked in the hole and saw Skunk. "Hand me up one of those dogs, my friend." The answer was, "No."

Then Coyote said, "Well, then. I will smoke you out of there." Skunk said, "What are you going to smoke me out with?" "I will use a weed." Skunk said, "I eat that kind of weed. I like it." Coyote said, "I will get some pine gum." Skunk replied, "Oh, you are going to kill me, are you?"

Coyote went to a pine grove and started collecting gum. He came back with it, stuck it into the hole, and started to make a fire. The smoke began to go into the hole. Skunk said, "Put some more on, you are killing me." While he said this, Skunk was coming close to the entrance of the hole. Coyote was blowing smoke down the hole. The smoke was beginning to roll now. "Keep on blowing," said Skunk. Coyote put his nose down and blew hard. Skunk was very close and he shot his smelly fluid right into Coyote's face and eyes so that he could not see. Skunk escaped all right.

—ACHIS

Coyote Tricked by Bug and Lizard

Coyote was roaming around. He found a little black stink bug on a tree and he went over to him. He was just going to eat him when Bug shouted, "Wait. Don't you want me to listen for you?" Coyote waited and Bug said, "I am listening. I hear someone coming who is going to kill you. I can see somebody coming who is going to kill you." Coyote was frightened and ran away without waiting to eat Bug.

Coyote came to a tree. He looked to see what was there and he saw a lizard. He was just going to eat it but Lizard said, "Wait. Don't do that. I am holding this pole that is bracing the earth. If I dropped it the earth would crack. I am tired. You hold it awhile, my friend. My arms are tired." Coyote said, "All right." He took the pole and held it while Lizard ran away. He held the pole tightly and thought, "The earth will break if I let go." His arms got tired. He shouted for help but Lizard was gone now. Then he thought, "I can't hold it another minute." He dropped it and ran as fast as he could. He looked back to see what had happened, but nothing at all happened. He went on his way.

—Achis

Bear Elopes with Mountain Lion's Wife

Bear ran away with Mountain Lion's wife. When Mountain Lion came home he missed his wife and started tracking her. He found their tracks and followed them. Bear and Mountain Lion Woman were resting. Bear took his shoes off. The woman was worried and said, "If my husband finds us, we are in danger." Bear said, "I am strong too." He rushed over to a bush and pulled it up to demonstrate his strength. "My husband is stronger than that."

The woman looked back and said, "There he comes, now." Bear grabbed his shoes but got them on the wrong feet. He jumped up and ran through the brush. You could hear the brush cracking. While Bear and Mountain Lion Woman had been resting, the woman said, "When are you going to have intercourse with me?" Bear replied, "I can't. I only have intercourse in the springtime."

When Mountain Lion found his wife he said to her, "What did Bear do to you? Did he have intercourse with you?" "No, he told me he only copulated in the spring. He did nothing to me." Mountain Lion went on top of the hill and waited for Bear to get there. Bear was all out of breath. He was puffing. He would look back now and then to see if anyone was following him. When he got close to Mountain Lion, he wrestled with him. He got him around the waist and threw him. He landed flat on his back. Since then Bears are flat on their backs. Mountain Lion went away and left Bear resting.

—Achis

Council on the Seasons

The birds and animals lived together. Coyote was the head man. He wanted to know how many winter months there should be. They said they wanted the winter to have many months. "Otter has thick fur," they said, "let there be as many winter months as there are hairs in Otter's fur." They said that if a baby were born in the winter, the winter would be so long that the baby would be an old man before summer came. Otter had thick fur. He said, "I don't want any of you little creatures to spoil what I see. I want things to be the way I want them." Someone said, "What is a person going to eat if the winter is so long?" Otter said, "I don't think they will starve. There will be plenty of snow they can eat. You know when you pack meat in rawhide bags that there are crumbs. When the snow is old and crusty, it is like those crumbs. You can eat that. I want all of you to agree. If anyone says no, I will fight him."

They stayed there day and night, trying to decide. A hawk with three toes sat by the door. At last they agreed with Otter. Hawk broke three sticks and threw them in front of Coyote. "There will be only three winter months," he said. Coyote chased that Hawk. He was chasing him to the hills. They came to some brush. Hawk took his eyes out and threw them in the brush. They turned into wild currants.

Coyote stopped at the berries and said, "All right, let's have it that way. We will have three winter months and I will add another to that and call it the 'buckskin end.' By the time winter is over the meat will be gone. During the winter the rawhide bags will soak up grease from the meat they contain. By March they will be cutting up the grease-soaked rawhide and eating that. That is why they will call the end of winter the buckskin end." They counted the hairs of all the animals and found that Otter had more than any other animal.

—Charlie Wash

The Corralled Buffalo

The Crows had plenty to eat. They had the animals locked up. The other people were starving. They used to say, "I wonder what they are doing over at Crow's camp." Whenever anyone went to Crow's camp to peek in through a hole in the tent, Crow would stick something in his eye. The Crow children used to play with a white ball. They always managed to get the white ball back. Darning Needle went to Crow's tent to peek in and when Crow poked something through the peephole, it slipped by him. Crow wondered what it was that he could not hurt. Darning Needle managed to look inside.

The people planned to move camp and leave one of their number behind, disguised as a dog. The Crow children found the dog and took him home to play with. Old Crow said, "It might be a little dog and it might be something else." They were afraid. The little dog was Weasel. That night Crow told the children to watch the dog, not to let him get away. The dog thought, "I wish they would all go to sleep." When the Crows were all asleep, Weasel let all the buffalo out. The Crows woke up and shouted, "He has let all our buffalo out. I knew he was not a dog." Weasel had let all the buffalo out except a few. Then he had run away.

—MORGAN GRANT

Bald Eagle

Bald Eagle never used to laugh. He was very serious. He had a bald head. When the people danced and had lots of fun, Bald Eagle never laughed. The people thought it was queer. Everyone else made jokes and laughed, but not Bald Eagle. The people thought, "We will make him laugh. We will dress and act funny."

They decorated Magpie. They painted him and put a

black g-string on him and told him, "You must dance right along in front of everyone in the circle." He was to dance the way he hops around now. Magpie went inside the circle. Everybody laughed at him. Finally Bald Eagle laughed. When he laughed, they noticed that his breath stank. It had a horrible smell. All the people crawled out under the tent. They found out why he never laughed. It was because his breath was so bad.

—MORGAN GRANT

Coyote Imitates a Woman

Coyote went with some women to pick berries. He was a man but he had put on a woman's dress and he carried a baby board on his back. They were on their way home and had stopped to dig some Indian potatoes when Coyote joined them. They looked up and saw a woman with a baby on her back. The women went to her and petted the baby. First one of them would take it, then another. One of the women took the baby out of the cradleboard and put it on her lap. The baby kept getting down between her legs and peeking. Another woman took the baby, but he did the same thing. "Why does it do that?" they said. The woman who had brought the baby said, "His aunt usually holds him. Perhaps she taught him to do that."

They camped for the night. Coyote said, "You women can have the baby sleep with you tonight." They all went to sleep. Coyote made them sleep soundly. Coyote got up and had intercourse with one of them, then another, until he had copulated with all of the women. He left their dresses up over their heads. Then he lay down not far off. One of the women woke up and said, "I knew that must have been Coyote. Look what he did to me." Then the others awakened and said, "He did it to me." "And to me." "He played with all of us." Coyote ran to a little hill and the women surrounded the hill. Coyote said, "I copulated with all of you." They hit him and he would dodge and yell the same thing at them. He got away.

—MORGAN GRANT

The Dogs' Council

The dogs were having a big council. They were all supposed to hang their anuses outside before they came in. They did this. Then they went into the tent and had a long talk. Someone shouted, "Fire!" They rushed out to where they had hung their anuses and grabbed any one and rushed off. Next morning they discovered that they did not have their own anuses and went around looking for their own. They are still looking. That is why dogs always smell each other's anuses.

—MORGAN GRANT

Water Babies

Water Babies cry like real babies. Mary has heard them down at Ouray. It was high water. She was in a menstrual hut. She heard the cry and said, "I wonder what baby that is?" She knew there was no one there. People are frightened when they hear the Water Babies.

—OLD MARY

Why Mules Are Sterile

There was a time when horses could talk. There were many horses. One mule was among them. A mare had a colt and all went to see it. It was very pretty and they were very proud of it. One of the last to come was Mule. Mule said, "That is one of the ugliest colts I have ever seen." Since then it never has any children. All the others admired the colt and that is why they have children. Mule wished the colt would never have any children, and that is why the mule never has colts itself.

—Lulu Chepoose

Why Dogs Don't Talk

Dog used to follow his master. The man used to go and get a girl and Dog would follow them and watch everything they did. When they went home, Dog told on his master. "Do you know what he did? He took a girl out." The man said, "You are always talking too much." He beat Dog. Dog got angry and said, "I will never talk again." He never has.

—Lulu Chepoose

The Cannibal Bird

Once there was a man with a little boy. The boy was going for water and he saw a pretty, young bird. His father said, "Go get him." The little boy ran after the bird and grabbed the bird. It grew into a big owl. It put the boy on its back and flew over the mountain with him. There was a big lake with an island. The bird took the boy to the island. There was an old woman there. When Owl got to the island he turned into a big man. He said to the old woman, "Kill the boy for me." The woman liked the little boy and she said, "You have food. There is some of that food you left here." Owl ate and drank. Every time he ate, he went to sleep.

He flew away and returned. He said, "Now you can kill that little boy." But the woman said, "No, you still have some food left." The old woman bruised her knee and made it bleed. She gathered that blood, it thickened, and she gave it to Owl to eat. She did this to save the little boy. Owl ate and drank and went away again. The old woman said to the little boy, "My grandson, I think we should kill Owl. You should practice shooting with your bow and arrows. After a while you will learn how." Owl had many bows and arrows and the little boy practiced with them. When the old woman thought Owl was coming, she cut her knee again and mixed the blood with some rocks that were finely ground.

Owl came and said, "I am hungry. Cook again." He wanted the little boy killed, but the woman kept saying that there was still some of his food left. She fed him what she had prepared. Owl began to get feverish and perspired. He grew very weak and crawled to his bed. She said to the boy, "Watch him carefully, my grandson." Owl went to the place where he usually drank. The little boy saw Owl's buttocks gaping open every now and then. The old woman said, "Now is your chance. Aim." The boy got his bow and arrow and shot Owl in the buttocks.

They wondered how they would escape. They were on an island in a big lake. They picked off Owl's feathers and tied them together to make a bridge from the island to the shore. The woman told the boy, "Cross that bridge. Go ahead." They crossed on the bridge to shore. The old woman said, "From which direction did he bring you?" "He brought me from this direction." It was not the same direction as the old woman's home, so they separated. The little boy reached his home safely and said, "Father." His father was blind. The old man said, "That sounds like my son. It is the way he used to talk." The boy kept calling, "Father." He discovered it was his own son and he wept. "My boy," he said. The little boy told how Owl had carried him off.

—CHARLIE WASH

The Boy Who Visited His Grandfather

Once there was a little boy and he was going to go visit his grandfather. His mother made him a sandbag suit so he would not be bitten by rattlesnakes. He wanted very much to visit his grandfather. His mother said, "I don't know how you are going to manage by yourself. It is a dangerous way." She made the suit to protect him. Then she fixed something for him to eat and told him, "Go along. Don't stay overnight in the desert. Go on and finally you will come to a big tree. Stand under that big tree. Stand up and sleep. Don't laugh. There will be something funny. There will be ghosts there and they will do funny things, but don't laugh or you will turn into a ghost."

The boy went on and on until he came to that tree. There was nothing else growing on the desert except that one tree. He stood under it. As soon as the sun went down, he heard people talking and laughing. They got close to him and he saw they were big-headed, snarly haired people. They saw the little boy and said, "What is this standing here in our playground?" They looked at him and said, "He has eyes." They poked him with their hands and tried to make him laugh, but he would not. They wrestled among themselves and did many funny things, but he would not laugh. They tormented him and spit in his eyes, but he said nothing. They said, "What kind of stick is this that grows here. It has eyes, it has a nose, but it does not say anything." They tormented the boy all night and at morning they disappeared.

The little boy continued on his journey. There were many prickly cacti on the ground and many rattlesnakes. The boy stepped over the cacti, but he stepped on some of the rattlesnakes as he went on. His mother had told him another place he would come to, a long hill. She had told him, "If you see a hole in the cliff, go in and look around. After you get inside there is a curve. That is the one I mean." The boy went on and looked for that cave and found it at last. He went in and sat down. It grew dark. When night came he was sitting there. Owl came along, kicking in the holes. The little boy could hear him. Owl came nearer and nearer. He kicked in the hole where the boy was. He could hear him stamping. Toward morning Owl flew away again.

His mother had told him to go on from there until he

came to a bunch of cedars. She told him to pick a strong tree and climb it. She told him to fix a strong seat in the branches so he would not roll off. He got there and found his tree. All the other trees had holes in them as though something had been digging in them. The boy had his bow and arrows. When he found the tree in which he was going to rest, he took one of his arrow points and stuck it in one of the holes. Then he climbed up and went to sleep. When he was sitting there, he heard something come along. It would hit and flop. When he saw it, he discovered it was a big animal with a rough hide. It came near, came under the boy's tree and sat down and grunted. It sat right on the arrow point. The arrow point killed it.

When the little boy climbed down in the morning, he saw this dead monster. Then he went on and reached his grandfather's place. The old man said, "They have been beating me at the Hand Game." The little boy asked who had been beating him. The grandfather said, "I don't know who they are. They come here in the evening. They have two feathers at the back of their heads."

Evening came and the old man told the little boy, "You can sit behind me tonight." They made a little peephole so the boy could see. The old man sat down with the little boy behind him. The people came, laughing and talking. The old man took the bones and started the game. They guessed right off and took the bones. The little boy behind his grandfather would tell the old man how to guess. The old man guessed well that night. His opponents said, "I wonder what is the matter tonight. He is guessing well. We usually beat him." They played all night and the old man won. They challenged him to another game the next night.

After they had gone the little boy said, "I know those people you played with. They are good to eat. They are jackrabbits. Their ears are those two feathers." Then the boy told the old man, "You better make a sack." He also told him to make a *pogamoggan*.

The boy said, "After they come, get up and go put the

sack with its mouth open in the doorway. Then come back, and after a while, tell one of the men to go make a fire. That will make them talk and they will tell you to make the fire yourself. Then you chase them with your *pogamoggan* and they will run for the door. They will run into the sack and we will get them."

The grandfather did as the boy told him. They played the game, and after a time the old man said, "Go make a fire." The others said, "Why do you want us to make a fire? You are winning." The old man chased them and they all ran into the sack. The old man got all of them and killed them.

—LULU CHEPOOSE

The Fool

There was a man who had a lot of pigs. He had a man working for him and he told him, "Herd those pigs. Don't let them get in the quicksand." The man was lazy and did not want to work. He did not herd the pigs. He sold them. When he returned in the evening he said to his master, "The pigs got in the quicksand while I was asleep." When he sold the pigs, he cut the ears off and threw them in the quicksand. The owner said, "I will go and see." He saw the ears and he pulled them. All he got was the ears.

The man worked for another master. He was told to get a load of wood. "Take this chain and tie the wood to the wagon." He got the wood and he tied the wood to the wheel of the wagon. The horses tried to pull but the wheel would not go round. He went back to his master and said, "I can't do it." The master said, "I did not tell you to do it that way. That is not the way. No wonder you are tired out."

Next morning he was told to unload the wagon and chop the wood. He chopped all the wood and then he chopped the wagon up. He said to the master, "I have finished chopping.

You better go see." He showed him the woodpile and there was the wood and the wagon, all chopped up.

His master told him to grease the wagon. He was given a whole can of axle grease. He greased the whole wagon frame. Then he went to the master and said, "The grease is all used up." The master said, "Why, I gave you a whole can!" The master went out and saw the whole wagon covered with grease.

—LULU CHEPOOSE

Siants (1)

Long ago there was a Siants. Two men went on a hunting trip. While they were hunting they were separated and lost each other. One man grew tired and hungry and thirsty. He made a fire. While he was sitting there by his fire he heard someone coming. It was a woman. She said, "What are you watching for?" He said, "I am hungry and thirsty. I know I am going to die. I have no water." The witch said, "I will get you a drink." She had her child with her. "Stay here and take care of your nephew."

The man thought, "I wonder what they sound like when they cry?" He pinched the little one's ear and it cried. The mother came back, breathing rapidly. She had heard the baby crying. "I know it is afraid of strangers," she said. Then she went away again. She had not gotten the water yet. While she was gone, the man stirred the fire and laid the baby in the coals. Then he ran back to camp.

When he got to camp he went in a *wickiup* and said, "Siants is after me." He told what he had done to the baby. The Siants came after him, but the people pulled him out through the rear of the tent and put him in another. They put him into a big rawhide bag. Siants said, "I saw his tracks going to this tent." She searched but could not find him, nor could she find tracks going anywhere. By this time the people

Women at Bitter Creek 1936. Alden Hayes.

had gotten their bows and arrows and they shot at Siants. Next morning they could not find Siants, but found the basket she had to pack the man in. They also found the arrow that shot her. During the night they had heard her groaning.

—Lulu Chepoose

Siants (2)

There was a little girl who never used to mind. Siants came and heard the little girl. Siants came to the door. She put out something white, her arm. The little girl reached for the white thing and Siants grabbed her. She put the little girl in her basket and took her away. Siants stopped to rest once in a while. When she sat down to rest, the child got out of the basket and put rocks in the basket.

Every time Siants rested, the child put in more rocks until the basket grew very heavy. The little girl defecated in the basket. The Siants had to go under a low branch of a cedar tree and the child grabbed the branch and pulled herself out of the basket. She ran home. When Siants got home, there was a fire ready for her. The old witch looked in the basket. There was nothing in it but feces. "What is this?" she said, and started in eating it. When the child got home she had learned a lesson and she was not naughty anymore.

—Lulu Chepoose

Many-Heads

There was once a man with three heads, one in the middle and one on each side of it. When anyone tried to kill him, they could not. He knew his visitors came to kill him, but he treated them well. He cooked human flesh and fed them. He would challenge them and say, "Come on, I am ready." They would fight with their knives. Three-heads always killed his opponent.

A man accompanied by a woman went to see him. They went in the house and Three-heads said, "Do you want to eat?" "No," said the man, "I don't want to eat." "All right," said Three-heads, "Let's go outside." He got his big knife and then they went outside. He sharpened his knife and rolled up his sleeves. The woman kept behind her man. She did not let Three-heads see her. The man said, "Don't go away from me. Stay right behind me." He got his knife out.

They fought. Three-heads did not kill his opponent this time. The man cut off one of Three-heads' heads. Then Three-heads said, "Wait a while and we will eat." He cooked. His neck was bleeding where one of the heads had been cut off.

The man said he did not want to eat. Three-heads ate and then challenged the man to fight again. He sharpened his knife again. They went out and fought. The man cut off another head. The woman stayed right behind him all this time. Three-heads wanted to stop and eat again. He cooked more meat. Then they went out to fight again. He had only one head left now and the man cut this off. He knocked him down. The head bounced around. Then he and the woman went home.

As they went along the road they met a Negro riding a burro. They thought, "We will watch and see what the Negro will do." The Negro saw Three-heads lying there and he went over and got off his burro and rolled in the blood. Then he jumped up and went away. He started talking aloud. "I went and killed Three-heads." The chief of the camp overheard him say this. The people rushed to the chief and said, "We better go see." They saw that the Negro was all bloody. The people went to Three-heads' camp and saw him lying dead. They believed that the Negro had killed him. The chief said to the Negro, "You can have my daughter for a wife." They said, "Put the Negro in water and soak him." They said, "Three-heads' people are coming after us."

The man who had killed Three-heads told the woman who was with him to go to camp. She was the chief's daughter.

Three-heads' people were angry because he had been killed. They came to fight with the Indians. They were brave and they were beating the Indians. The man who killed Three-heads got on a white horse and rode out and killed most of the attackers. Things were quiet for a while, but then Three-heads' people returned and killed many Indians. The man came out on a pinto horse this time and chased the enemy away. The chief said, "I wonder who that man is. He always comes to the rescue in the nick of time. I would like to know who he is. He is the only one that can drive off the enemy. He rides a pinto horse, but I don't know who he is." The chief's daughter said, "I know who he is. He is the man who killed Three-heads." "What about the Negro?" said the chief. The girl said, "The Negro just said that. After my man killed the monster, the Negro came and found Three-heads dead. He went and rolled in the blood." The chief said, "Where is he now?" "He went in this direction."

They hunted for him. They looked but they could not find him. Finally they saw a big pile of manure. They said, "This is the only place we have not looked." They looked and there he was. They took him to the chief. The chief asked, "Did you kill Three-heads?" "Yes." The woman said, "Yes, he killed him." The chief told them to throw away the man who was soaking. So they dragged the Negro out of the water.

They were afraid that Three-heads' people were coming to fight again. They did come and fight. The man came out on his horse and killed them one by one until they were all dead.

—CHARLIE WASH

White River Tales

Men at White Rocks, 1909. Edward Sapir. Marriott Library Special Collections.

The Origin of Death

Wolf wanted women to be pregnant in their arms and suffer no pain, but Coyote said, "Let them bear children in their abdomens and suffer lots of pain."

Wolf wanted the dead buried in anthills and wanted them to come to life again next day, but Coyote said, "No, let them be put in the ground and let families all cut their hair and be sad and cry."

Wolf wanted no winter, wanted it always to be nice weather, but Coyote said, "No, let it be cold part of the time."

—Lincoln Picket

Rabbit and Moon

The moon used to be a man who had a face. The moon rolled all over where all the birds and animals were and killed lots of them. It used to be all fire, all hot. All the animals were killed except Rabbit. He said, "Hide some place quickly, the moon with catch you and burn you up." He hid under the rabbit-brush and nowadays rabbits hide under that brush. Rabbit got brown marks on his back where he was scorched by the moon.

—Pearl Perika
(Stella LaRose, translator)

Pearl Perika. Alden Hayes.

Cottontail Shoots the Sun

Cottontail was a person. A long time ago the sun used to be hot, hotter than it is today. Cottontail got mad at it because it was so hot. Away over the hill where the sun rose, they used to go and watch. When the sun saw the spies trying to get him, he would come around the side of the hill and not get caught. Cottontail was angry and was going to see what he could do. He told his family he was going to go to the sunrise and he went.

While he was journeying he hunted other rabbits. Cottontail had two names, his ordinary one, Tawuc, and a "good" (formal) name. A weed called him by his ordinary name and he got angry and hit the weed with his club. Cottontail used to be very busy and they would ask him why he hit that man and he would say, "Because he called me 'Tawuc.'"

As he was journeying, he saw someone digging. When he arrived there he found Bear making a place for the winter. Cottontail said, "What are you doing?" Bear replied, "I heard Tawuc was coming and that he was mad and killing people right and left. I am going to dig a home here so when Tawuc comes I will have a place to hide. When I see him coming I will make a beeline for my hole and hide in it." Cottontail said, "Show me how you are going to do this." So the Bear said, "This is how I am going to do it." He pretended Rabbit was coming and he ran and jumped into his hole. Then Cottontail said, "What are you going to hear that will make you do that?" "Oh, when I hear Cottontail coming, I will jump into my hole and hide." Cottontail wanted him to do it again. The last time he ran into the hole Cottontail said, "Aren't you going to peek out before you get all the way in?" And Bear said, "Yes. Like this." And he poked his head out of the hole and Cottontail hit him with his club and then went on.

He continued his journey and met two little boys. He asked them where their mother was and they said they had no mother. She had been out gathering wild carrots and a big rock did not want her to have any so he rolled on her and killed her. Cottontail asked, "What do you live on? What do you eat?" "Oh, we eat anything we can get." Cottontail asked, "What do you make fire of?" The boys said, "We do not make fire because when we go over to the bush it makes a funny noise and we are frightened." Cottontail said, "What do you drink?" "Oh, we never drink because when we go to the creek the water splashes on us and frightens us."

Cottontail said, "You go get some of those sticks you said were mean." They all went together. When the boys touched the bush, sparks flew out and hit their faces and made big blisters. Cottontail got mad and beat the bush and said, "One of these days you're not going to be mean. Even old women will be able to get you." After Cottontail beat the bush he told the boys to gather the wood and said it would no longer hurt them.

Cottontail sent them to get water. When the boys got a dipperful, the water rushed after them. Cottontail hit the water and beat it and said, "You will never be mean again after this. Anybody can drink you. Any old woman can come and get you."

Cottontail asked the little boys if they ever heard anyone say Tawuc was coming. The boys said yes, but they used his good name, and Cottontail was glad because that was the name he liked. He called the boys grandsons. He asked, "Where is the rock that killed your mother?" They told him and they went there. Cottontail told the boys to go away and not to look back to watch what he did. One boy kept wanting to look back and the other boy said, "No, Grandfather said not to look back." When that boy looked back he could see Cottontail way under, trying to push the rock up. The boy could see Cottontail's anus, his tail was sticking up. Finally he did get the rock off and the woman said, "Oh, I have had the best sleep." She got up and went to her sons. She got the roots she was after and they went home and had something to eat. They were the Dove family.

Cottontail went on toward the sunrise. He just barely got there. There was someone camped nearby. Cottontail said, "I often wonder how I can catch the sun. Every time I get there the sun always sees me and sneaks up on the other side. Here is where I aim to be. This is my journey's end. When the sun comes up, it has the brightest eyes. It can see all over. I never can hide."

So Cottontail went on up the hill, found a hole and waited there for the sun to come. Sure enough, the sun came up and it had big bright eyes and it saw Cottontail, so it went to one side of him. It did not come right over him as Cottontail wanted it to. Cottontail said, "Oh, the sun saw me this morning." He asked another man if he knew any way of getting the sun and the man said, "I don't believe the sun would see me because I can put my web over me." This man was Spider. So Spider made a web by the rabbit hole and sat under there. Sun came up again the next morning and did not see Cottontail under the spider web. Sun was just coming up and had not seen Cottontail hiding there and Cottontail hit the sun with his club and that set the world on fire. Everything burned around there and Cottontail ran back with the fire burning behind him.

Cottontail said, "Who will help me?" He wanted to know what to do. The trees said they would be nothing but ashes and the water said it would boil. Cottontail asked everything but he could find nothing to protect him. Even the ground was too hot. He said all the rest of the things were going to burn except one little weed that looked like rabbitbrush and he said, "Will you burn up too?" The brush said, "No, fire will just go over us and we will make a noise." So Cottontail dug under the brush and just got under it when the fire came. It passed over the brush and Cottontail was saved. The brown spots behind the rabbits' ears are where Cottontail got scorched that time.

Everything got burned up and when people see black rocks they said, "Oh, this is what got burned when Cottontail set the world on fire."
[They used to tell these stories at night and the young folks would get so sleepy. Then they would quit.]

—Archup
(Stella LaRose, translator)

Tricking an Enemy

One man and his wife were camped all alone. They went to bed one night. The woman said, "I hear something crossing the river. I hear water splashing." The man said, "Oh, you're always talking about something dangerous." In the morning the woman got up and said, "Last night you told me that noise was just the water making a noise like a man and woman feeling that they want intercourse. But look, this is what I was thinking. Get up and face them." The man peeped out from under the robes and saw the strangers. Then the man said, "Now that they are eating, you better go out and get that big piece of fat out there. Get our ropes and bridles and hide them somewhere."

The woman went out and hid the bridles and ropes and brought back the fat. He put it over the flames and melted it.

When it got to melting and dripping he told his wife to leave the tent. She left. The man took the fat and threw it in the faces of the enemy and burned them. Then he ran out of the tent. They got their horses and mounted and ran away from the enemies.

This is a true story.

—ARCHUP

(Stella LaRose, translator)

The Crows That Went Visiting

The Black Crows were people. Some of the Crows would go visiting and never come back. So Black Crow thought he would go see what happened to them. He went on his journey. He met an old woman who was camped there. He asked the old woman where visitors went. She said, "Oh, there are lots of camps, but that one in the middle is where visitors go. It is our leader's camp." So he went there, knocked at the door, and went in. The leader and his family were in the tent, his daughter on one side of him. Crow sat beside the daughter and laid his bow and arrows alongside him. The chief said to his daughter, "You better get him some supper." Old Crow was a medicine man.

He ate his supper. It was getting late but he still sat there. While he was eating supper the old woman and her daughter left the tent. The old woman said that she was afraid of Crow, but she told her daughter that she might as well go to bed with him. Crow was listening and he heard. When they came back, the chief told his daughter to make the bed and make it big enough for two. She did this and she and Crow went to bed together. Crow went to sleep and slept soundly. He woke up in the night very sick. He vomited and the chief woke up and heard him. He told his daughter to get up, make a fire, do something. Crow was a sick man.

The chief used to feed visitors and then send them to bed with the girl. What Crow vomited was all worms and nasty things, that is what the chief had fed him. Crow said, "I always get sick when I lay my head in the middle of the tents." Then the chief called out to all the people, "This visitor says he always gets sick when he lays his head in the middle of the tents. You better move your tents from the back." So they all moved their tents from the back and left an opening way down the line. Then the chief said, "Why don't you move your bed outside." The girl moved the bed out, and she and the sick man went to bed outside.

Early in the morning, just at daylight, Crow said, "I better go and hunt where my father used to hunt. I'll go there and hunt." He said, "When your father asks where I am, you tell him I went hunting." He went flying off alone. He built a big brush pile, leaves and brush. On top of it he stuck an animal's tongue on a stick. Then he went back again in the evening.

He said, "I killed a buffalo and I want you all to go with me and see it. Everybody must come, all the children too." So the chief announced what he said and told all the people to get ready to go on a journey to where Crow had killed the buffalo. Crow slept outside again that night. He said, "We have a long journey to make. There is a big hill, then another hill and another and away out on the plains you can see that big, dead animal."

Next morning they all packed up and went. Crow told them the way to go. He was not going with them. He wanted to search for his people who had come visiting and never returned. Crow flew fast to see if the people got there, and he saw them when they stopped at the first hill. When they got over the last hill they stopped and looked and they saw the place where the big brush pile was. "That's it," they said. The chief's wife and daughter had stayed at home. When the people got to the brush pile, they started throwing the brush and leaves and could not find any buffalo, just the tongue. That is how Crow fooled them. They were mad. They started back. Crow said, "You go that way and I will go around this way and maybe I will kill something."

Archup and family, White River, 1936. Alden Hayes.

Just as Crow got over the hill he made a noise like a gun shooting and the people came running to see what had been killed. He had fooled them. He told them to go on home and said, "I may kill something." As soon as Crow got out of sight he again made a noise of a gun shooting and they thought, "He is just fooling us again." They would not go to see. Crow was mad and he caused a big flood and it rained for days right over these people and they were all wet.

Crow flew home to his wife. Then he went back and slept with the chief's daughter that night, but then he killed her and his mother-in-law too, because he was a doctor and he knew that it was the chief who had fed the visitors the stuff that killed them. He had not died like the others because he was a doctor. The people that he killed with the flood were camp robbers (Rocky Mountain jays).

—ARCHUP
(Stella LaRose, translator)

The False Friend

Coyote stole Winter's wife. They traveled all the time. It was very cold. Winter used to be a person. Winter tracked Coyote and his wife. They would stop some place for a little while, but Winter followed them. They made a fire and left. When Winter got there, there were still ashes in the fireplace. Winter followed their tracks and caught them where they had made their tent. The wind came and blew Coyote out into the ashes. Winter blew him into the ashes and took away his wife.

That's all.

—PEARL PERIKA
(Stella LaRose, translator)

Frog and Eagle

A long time ago Frog had a daughter. She said to her father, "I saw the handsomest man on this earth. He has better hands than yours, they are not spotted like yours." Her father said, "Bring me something. I will wash my hands and then I bet I will be the better man." She put some water beside him for him to wash his hands with and she laughed at him. He said, "Let us go and see that man." They went.

The handsome man was sitting down. It was Eagle. Frog said, "Let's go down to where I used to peep a long time ago." They went together. Frog was the meanest man of the bunch. Frog said, "I used to peep like this through the rocks all the time." He told Eagle, "You peep in," and Eagle did. Frog pushed him down and he flew around inside that deep rock. He came out by another hole and came over behind Frog, where Frog was looking in the hole to see where Eagle had gone to. Eagle pushed Frog down and killed him. Eagle said that anyone who tried to save Frog would be a frog. No more people, he will be called frog now, so now he is in the water going, "quag, quag." They all went into the water and became frogs.

—Pearl Perika
(Mamie Alhandra, translator)

Coyote and the Berries

Coyote was sitting by the side of the water. He looked in the water and saw berries down there, hanging down over his head. He reached down in the water to get the berries and all he got was mud. He tried again and put his hand way down and he fell in. His buckskin pants got all wet and when they dried they stuck to his skin. He tried to pull them off and pulled all his skin off, poor old fellow.

—Pearl Perika
(Mamie Alhandra, translator)

The Hoodwinked Dancers

Wood Rat called all the animals to come and dance. Wood Rat had a spear. He called to all the animals who lived in the mountains and all those who lived on the plains. "Come and Wood Rat will give you a song and you will dance. Kai kai," is what he sang. He got all the animals to shut their eyes while he sang. Wood Rat kept his eyes open and his spear in his hand. He sneaked up on the best and fattest animal and speared him. Then he told the animals to run, and they opened their eyes and ran.

After a while they discovered that they were getting fewer in number, that the best among them were gone. "What is happening?" they said. Then they came back again. They had a little animal that was carried on the back of its mother. They told this baby to keep his eyes open to watch what Wood Rat did. Wood Rat came to the sister of this baby and the little animal yelled and said, "Sister, he is coming for you!" They all opened their eyes and ran.

Buffalo chased Wood Rat and Rat went into his hole. Buffalo pawed him out and he ran for a tree. Buffalo destroyed the tree but Wood Rat got away. He ran into a hole in the rock but Buffalo destroyed the rock and hooked Wood Rat in his side, and he ran away with his insides hanging out. Buffalo thought that Wood Rat was dead, but he got home and Coyote came and fixed up his wound.

When Coyote came in he called Rat "friend." He saw all the meat that was hanging up in Wood Rat's hole. Coyote cut off the piece of Wood Rat's intestine that was hanging out and put a piece of rawhide over the wound. Rat's wife cooked all kinds of meat and Coyote ate it up. Coyote said, "So that is how you kill them." Rat paid Coyote for curing him by feeding him.

Coyote said he was going to try to get some meat the same way that Rat did. Coyote said he was going to call all the people, but Rat said he did not think the trick would work again. Coyote went to the same place and called all the people to come dance. He sang the same song that Wood Rat did. Then they all came and Coyote told them to shut their eyes. The same baby on his mother's back kept his eyes open. Coyote sang the same song that Rat did and told the people to shut their eyes. All the people were onto the trick and they all ran away and he didn't get one.

—Archup
(Stella LaRose, translator)

The Buffalo

Coyote and his family played snowballs and fought with snowballs with Crow's children. Crows were in a camp just a little way off. One of the snowballs was a ball of kidney fat. Coyote's children thought it was a snowball but it was not. Coyote's children were hungry, but they took the ball to their father and showed it to him. "This is what they were fighting with." It was harder than snowballs.

Coyote called all his family together at his place. He said it was no wonder the Crows were hollering, they had something to eat. Coyote wanted to know which one of his family would spy on the Crows. In the evening Crow's family were hollering again, and one of Coyote's family peeked through a hole in the tipi. They all saw the eye in the hole from inside and hit at it and he ran away without seeing anything.

One of the little blue bugs, a Darning Needle, was asked to go down and find out what made the Crows so gay. He said he would go. He went down and kept right on looking even though the Crows did jab at his eye. There was a big rock by the fireplace and there was something being taken from there. Crow was feeding his children with this. So Darning Needle went and told Coyote and Coyote said, "That is what they have been doing all this time, eating. No wonder they are so gay." So Coyote said, "Tomorrow morning early we will move camp before the buffalo gets around, for we are hungry and we have to get something to eat."

He asked which one of his people wanted to stay at the old campground. He said whoever stayed would have to disguise himself as a little dog that had been left behind. They asked Weasel if he would go and see Coyote. He went to see Coyote. They still had that snowball made of fat, and they asked Weasel if he would like to stay at camp and watch Crows. Weasel said he would be the little dog and would stay around when the rest went on.

Next morning they all went except Weasel, and he stayed there like a little dog. As soon as they left, the Crow children all came out and they saw the cute little puppy and took him home. He was making a noise like a puppy. So they took the puppy home with them. Old Mother Crow said, "What a cute little puppy."

In the evening they all started making a noise again and they fed the puppy but he would not eat. Night came. The puppy played around. The child that found the puppy wanted to sleep with him but the puppy wouldn't stay still, he kept crawling about. Finally all the Crows were asleep and the puppy got up. He was full of gas and he broke wind. They breathed in the smell and then they could not wake up. The puppy went to the rock and under the rock were lots of buffalo and the puppy set them all free. Finally all got out of the hole under the rock except one old cow who was still there when Mother Crow woke up.

The puppy followed Coyote's tracks to tell him the news. He told Coyote that under that rock were a lot of buffalo, and he had set them all free. Coyote said, "Thank you, my friend." Coyote was so glad that he could not go to sleep. All the buffalo were free. He wanted morning to come so they could all make bows and arrows. There were many buffalo there, they were thick as trees. It looked like a valley of cedar trees but the trees were buffalo.

Next morning came and they all made their bows and arrows out of wild currant bush. Old Woodpecker was making arrow points out of flint and they all traded with him for points. Coyote just took a leaf of quaking aspen to use for his points. Next evening he called again and wanted to know if they were all ready to go out and hunt. They all said they had their bows and arrows ready, so he said, "Tomorrow we go hunt for our meat." He was so anxious he could not sleep all night. He wanted morning to come.

He got them all up early to get their horses ready. He took his wife along on another horse. They went way up in the plains where buffalo were thick as cedar trees in a valley. Coyote made his people get on the horses they had been leading. Coyote had a fast-running horse. He said, "We each have a chance to get our own meat. We are not going to give meat to one another. We will not share our meat." So they all took after the buffalo on their horses. Coyote's arrow points would not go through the buffalo, they just bent. No buffalo dropped when he hit it. He could not kill any buffalo. Everybody else had some. His wife came along and wanted to know what had happened. She asked him why he had not gotten any buffalo. "Well," he said, "my arrows just broke."

Another man was nearby butchering, and they went down and looked at him. He asked Coyote how many buffalo he got. Coyote said, "None." The other man said, "You said yourself we could not get any meat from other people, we had to get our own." But he gave Coyote a piece of meat to take home.

When they got home Coyote went to make some more arrows. He went over to Woodpecker. He would not buy or trade any, he kept grabbing at the points and Woodpecker pushed him away. Coyote got mad and went home without any points. He went home and got his club. He returned and sat and he grabbed again, but Woodpecker would not let him have any. He hit Woodpecker with his club and knocked him unconscious and stole all the points. Then Coyote went home.

Next morning Coyote was ready to hunt and he wanted them all to go hunting again. This time he said, "We are all going to give to one another. We will share our meat." They took out after the buffalo and Coyote killed them on all sides. His wife came and Coyote was very proud of all the buffalo he had killed. He was the only one who killed any that day and he had to divide with all the rest of them.

—ARCHUP

(Stella LaRose, translator)

The Coyote and the Women

Coyote was going along one day when he heard a lot of women singing and laughing up on top of a cliff. He wanted to see those women, but he did not know how he was going to get to them. Finally he decided to try to climb the cliff. It was awfully steep and he had a hard time, but he just had to get to those women who were laughing and having such a fine time up there. They knew he was trying to climb up and they just wished he would fall.

He got almost to the top when, sure enough, he did slip and fall way down to the bottom and he broke his leg, poor old fellow. The women saw him fall and they ran down to him. When they saw he had a broken leg they were sorry for him and took turns packing him on their backs. So Coyote got to those women after all, even if he had to break his leg to do it.

—STELLA LaROSE

Coyote Seeks a Name

Coyote wanted a name for his little son, so he went over to see the Woodchucks to see if they had a good one. Coyote asked the names of all the Woodchuck children. One little fellow, just about the size of Coyote's son, had a real cute name. Coyote liked it and asked if he could have the name for his son. Woodchuck said yes and Coyote started home with the name.

He had not gone very far when he stumbled and fell and when he got up he had lost the name. So back he went to the Woodchucks to get the name again. They told him again and Coyote started home. He got a little farther this time before he stumbled and fell and lost the name again. So back he went once more, poor old fellow. He started home again, and again he fell and lost the name and had to go back. This happened several times till Coyote was ashamed to go back again and went home without any name for his son.

—STELLA LaROSE

Trickster Marries His Daughter

Coyote had a family, a wife and children. One tooth was
pulled out of his mouth for each member of his family; one for
his wife and one for each of his children. He used to hunt rabbits with his littlest boy. Coyote would go on one side of a big
rock and his son would go on the other. They cornered the
rabbit under the rock. They made a noise to call the rabbits.
While they were hunting rabbits, Coyote stepped on a rabbit
bone and his leg swelled up. He grew sick. "When I die," he
said, "you folks should put me on a cedar. Be sure and make
a fire under the cedar. When you make a fire, go away and
leave me. Where you go you will meet many people. When
you see a man on a white horse, be sure you give our oldest
daughter to him. Let him marry her. When you leave me,
don't any of you look back."

The littlest boy who used to go hunting with Coyote kept
coaxing his mother to let him look back, but she was frightened and would not let him. Finally she thought he was far
enough away and he looked back. He said, "Oh, my father
moved. He rolled off that cedar." His mother said, "Oh, you
are crazy, your father could not move. Your father is dead."

They went on a journey. They found some people
camped and they camped with them. After they were settled, they met a man on a white horse, a fine proud man.
"There is the man my father said I should marry," said
Coyote's oldest daughter. The man on the white horse rode
over to a little knoll. Coyote's wife said, "There is the man
your father wanted you to marry."

That evening the man came to their camp and sat down.
They all talked. Coyote's wife said, "All right. We will all go
to bed. This is the man your father wanted you to marry and
you better take him for your husband." So Coyote's daughter
went to bed with the man.

They camped there a while. Coyote's wife said, "Your
father knew a good place to hunt rabbits. Let us go and get
some rabbits. I am hungry for some rabbit meat. We will take

Wringing hide at Archup's camp. Alden Hayes.

this fine proud man with us. So they all went on a rabbit hunt. Coyote's wife said to her little boy, "Show this man the places where your father used to hunt." They went hunting. The little boy made the noise to call the rabbits just as he used to do for his father. They went hunting several times. The last time the boy was on one side of a big rock and his brother-in-law was on the other side. He looked at his brother-in-law and he saw the gaps in his mouth where there were teeth missing. He said, "That man is just like my father. He has the same teeth missing as my father had."

The little boy ran home and said to his sister, "You have your father for your husband." His mother said, "What is he saying?" The little boy repeated, "She has her father for her husband." The mother said to the daughter, "When your father had intercourse with me, he always kissed me on the cheek." The daughter said, "That is what my husband does."

So they all ran away from there. They went straight up. When the man finished hunting, he returned home. He searched all over for his family. Then he looked up in the sky and there he saw them. He said, "Someday people will call you Seven-Stars-Together" (Pleiades). They called back and said, "You will be only a coyote, snooping and smelling around." That is how Coyote was separated from the members of his family.

—Archup

(Stella LaRose, translator)

The Bungling Host

Coyote visited Beaver. He said, "Hello, my friend." Beaver said, "I don't know what to feed you. I have nothing for you to eat." He killed one of the beaver children and then he killed another, the smallest one. The meat was cooked for Coyote. Beaver said to Coyote, "Don't lose any of the bones. Gather all the bones and put them together." When he finished eating, Beaver gathered up the bones and dumped them into the water. As soon as he did this they turned into beavers and there were many beavers swimming around.

When Coyote was leaving he invited Beaver to come and visit him some day. Next morning Beaver got up and said that he could not think of any reason for visiting Coyote. His wife said, "Well, he invited you to go see him. You ought to go and see him." Beaver went to Coyote's home. Coyote said to him, "Well, my friend, I have nothing to feed you." Then he did just as Beaver had done. He seized two of his children and killed them. He cooked the meat and put it in front of Beaver. Beaver said, "No, I do not eat at anyone's home." So Coyote ate his own children, but he kept all the bones and put them together. Then he took the bones to the creek just as Beaver had done. Beaver said, "I hope the leavings do not swim around as mine did." Sure enough, the bones sank right down to the bottom of the river.

—Archup

(Stella LaRose, translator)

Coyote's Brother Cured

Coyote's brother was sick. They tried all the doctors but he did not seem to get any better. A bird (a large bird, like an eagle, with dark feathers and red head, which flies when the wind blows) was sent for to doctor Coyote's brother. He came when he was sent for and he doctored that night. He said, "How are you? How do you feel?" The patient said, "Oh, I get out of my head and I see ducks, ducks, ducks." He was accusing Duck of being the one who had caused the illness.

The doctor said to the patient, "Get up and go get some water from the middle of the pond." The patient got up and went off, but he did not go to the middle of the pond for the water. He got the water from the edge of the pond and took it to the doctor. The doctor knew it was not from the middle of the pond, so he sent the patient back to bring water from the middle of the pond. The patient brought some more water. This time he got it from a short distance from shore. The doctor looked at it and told him to go back and bring water from the middle of the pond. The water was so deep that the man was afraid to go out to the middle of the pond. This time, however, he did go to the middle. He thought he would sink, but he dipped up some water and got back to shore. The doctor said, "This is water from the middle of the pond. I know the patient is sick. I know what caused it. He got the disease from the Duck Woman. She is the cause of it. I am going to cure him." Next morning after the doctor had gone, the patient got up and was all right.

—Archup

(Stella LaRose, translator)

The Curious Man

A man called to a group that there was a large mountain sheep on the hill. He asked another man to go with him to see it. All those that were going to hunt the mountain sheep went up on the hill. These two men went too. All the people were looking and said, "Look at him. There he is." He was a big snake curled up among the rocks. Most of the people could see him. Some could not see and they would say, "Do you see him right there?" "No, I don't see him." They went back home and said that they would return the next day. Next morning they said, "Get ready, we will go get him today." They said to the man, "Do you see him today?" and he replied, "Oh, yes. Look at his horns sticking up. There he is. That is what they are looking at." Snake really had horns.

They came back to see him again. One of the men was a snake charmer and Snake did not hurt anyone because the snake charmer was there. Snake lived in a big cave. The people arrived there before sunrise. They dug a big hole. Snake came out. The ground was bare where Snake crawled. On Snake's tail there were many bells. When he came out into the sunrise the bells on his tail rang beautifully. He came to where he usually curled up and he went round and round and the two men (the snake charmer and the man) were frightened. They said, "We will wait until he goes to sleep." The snake charmer said, "He is asleep now." They kept on digging a hole.

In the afternoon Snake awoke and uncoiled and went back to his hole in the rocks. They covered the hole they had dug with sticks. They made loopholes through which to shoot their arrows. They said, "We will come back tomorrow and try to kill him."

The young man went to his wife and said, "What do you think I saw? It was not what they said it was. It was big Snake with bells on his tail." His wife was so frightened she shook.

Next morning they went out again and hid in the trap, and the curious man went with them. Someone had to watch. The brave ones went into the hole. Just as the sun was rising, big Snake came crawling out, making a pretty sound with his bells. His horns were beautiful as he sat there. The people in the pit waited for him to go to sleep. When the sun got a little higher up, the snake charmer said, "He is asleep now." They began to shoot their arrows at him, but Snake did not move. They got a lot of arrows in him. Soon he began to move. He uncoiled himself and went round and round, with his bells singing. He came right over the top of the dugout where the people were hiding, and he brushed the dirt off the top with his tail. They cried out, "He is going to kill us all." The curious one was frightened. The covering of the pit began to give way under the weight of Snake. But Snake quieted down, his tail did not move so swiftly.

The man said, "I think he is dead." They got out of the pit and examined Snake. He was dead. He was the biggest thing they had ever seen. One of the men said, "I will cut his head off." So he cut off his head and then they cut up Snake as you would slice a roll of meat and gave a piece to each person. They asked the curious man if he ate that kind of meat and he said he did not, so he was not given a piece. The rest of them took their pieces home, including the head with its horns and the tail with the bells.

Snake was a poisonous snake. If a person got a whiff of his breath, he would be killed. He would froth at the mouth. They were not harmed when they killed Snake because of the presence of the snake charmer.

Someone asked the curious man to go with him to see something else. Next morning they all went to see another big monster. The monster went to the rocks. They said, "Look where he went. Look at his tracks." They went after him. It was only the tracks of Porcupine. They killed him. They had made the curious man think it was a big monster and it was only old Porcupine. They all took a piece of the meat. They asked the curious man whether he liked that kind of meat and when he said, "Yes," they gave him a piece of meat. He took it home and his wife fixed it.

Next morning they said that they had seen something by the river. His friend said to the curious man, "Shall we go see?" They went down there and the people said, "Here he is. He is lying down. He is a big fellow, the biggest one we have ever seen." When they saw the monster it turned out to be nothing but Water Snake. They killed him and each got a piece, but the curious man did not eat snake.

Next morning somebody reported another monster and when they went to see it, it was only Toad. "Look at him, isn't he big?" They killed Toad and all took a piece of him except the curious man.

This is a fairy story. The man is real.

—ARCHUP

(Stella LaRose, translator)

Winter's Wife

Wind had a wife. He left his wife. She married Winter. Once, when Winter was out hunting, Rabbit stole his wife and married her. She had three children very shortly after. Every day they moved their camp, but Winter could see where they had made a huge fire. Winter followed them, but they kept on moving camp. Each time he would see where they had made a fire, but they had gone. Rabbit and the woman camped. They built a house. Winter came and blew hard. It grew cold. Rabbit slept on the south side of the tipi with his wife and children. They were very cold. They guessed that Winter was getting close to them. Winter went under the tipi at the spot where the woman was lying and blew Rabbit into the fire. Rabbit tried to hide under the woman's dress before Winter blew him into the fire. He was cold. Winter blew him into the fire. He died. This is why Rabbits always die in February.

Winter remarried his wife. Rabbit's children were dead and cold. Winter said, "Why did you marry this Rabbit? Throw his children outside. They will be called rabbits."

Winter had had two children by this woman. He said, "Why didn't you take care of my children? You let them get dirty. You took care of Rabbit's children. Rabbit's children will all die. They will be called rabbits and everyone will kill and eat them."

—PEARL PERIKA
(Mamie Alhandra, translator)

Coyote's Adventures

Coyote heard some children talking on the path ahead of him. He said to the children, "Where is your mother?" They told him she had gone down a certain path. He said, "Whose children are you?" and they told him they were Sage Hen's children. Coyote stood there for a while and then he urinated over the children.

When their mother returned she asked them what they had been doing and complained of the way they smelled. They told her Coyote was responsible for that. She asked which direction Coyote had taken and she flew after him. He was way down the river by the beaver dams. He was wearing pine-bark leggings. They were pretty white leggings. Sage

Mamie and Sam Alhandra [upper left] and Pearl Perika (Mamie's mother) [lower right]. Alden Hayes, 1936.

Hen flew in front of him and hid by a place where he would have to pass. When he was near she flew up suddenly making a great noise. Coyote was frightened and fell into the water. He nearly drowned. One of the sticks in the beaver dam stuck in his side. He crawled out of the water and took off his leggings to dry them. His side hurt him.

While he was waiting for his leggings to dry, Muskrat came down the river. Coyote said to him, "Oh, my brother, someone chased me and nearly caught me, but I got away. However, they wounded me. Can you fix it?" So Muskrat rubbed his side until he brought the edges of the wound together and healed it. As soon as Coyote was well, Muskrat was frightened of him and he dashed into the water. When he got to the other side of the river, Coyote called him to come back. Muskrat did not trust him and refused to come. Coyote became angry and called him all kinds of names. He mocked his funny tail, his eyes, his appearance. Muskrat grew angry and jumped into the river and swam away.

Coyote took his white leggings, which were dry now, and tried to soften them as he would buckskin, by rubbing them together. He rubbed and rubbed and the leggings came to pieces. He had no leggings.

As he was going down the side of the river, he saw something dark. When he got closer he saw it was Bear, digging roots. He went and lay down in the tall grass near her and said, "What are you doing?" "I am digging roots to eat," Bear said. Coyote made fun of Bear and said, "You are a funny-looking person. You have big buttocks and little ears. You have funny little genitals hanging out there." Bear grew angry and charged him. Coyote jumped up and ran away. Bear chased him. She drew near. Coyote was getting weak. Bear touched him on the buttocks and he urinated. Coyote saw a big rock and ran around it, but Bear was right behind him.

While he was running he saw some buffalo horns, and he picked them up and turned and charged Bear. When she saw the horns she was frightened and turned and ran. Coyote now chased Bear. He kept sticking the horns in her buttocks, and every time he did this she urinated. Then they got back to the place where Bear had been digging roots and they sat down and rested. Coyote said, "I nearly died laughing when I chased you. Every time I stuck you, you urinated." Bear said, "You, too, looked very funny. You did the same thing when I chased you." They laughed to think how funny they looked.

Coyote told her he was on his journey following his brother when he met her. He went on following his brother's trail. He could see the marks where they dragged their tent poles. They went to the top of a hill. Coyote saw a large boulder and he saw all kinds of jewelry around this rock—beads, rings, and other jewelry. These were gifts that people had given to the rock. Coyote picked up some beads and thought, "What a handsome man I am." He thought how proud he

would be when people saw him with all this handsome
jewelry.

He kept on his way, following the tracks. He heard
something behind him; it sounded as though something had
fallen. He looked back and saw that big boulder chasing him.
He thought, "I will go straight up this high hill and Rock will
not be able to follow me up there." He looked back and there
was Rock following him right up the hill. It followed through
the thick brush, up the steep places. It went everywhere he
went. He was tired.

He knew he had taken the things that belonged to Rock.
He removed the jewelry and threw the things back at Rock.
He said, "If I have anything belonging to you, here it is. Quit
following me." But Rock kept right on following him. Coyote
saw a big cottonwood tree and he went to it. He asked it to
help him. The tree said, "I will help you. Get behind me." He
did. Rock came straight for the tree. It hit the tree, which
broke, and Coyote had to run on.

He went across the flats with Rock after him. He saw a
dark spot that turned out to be an eagle, and he said, "Help
me, protect me. Rock is chasing me." "All right," said Eagle.
"Get behind me." Rock hit Eagle and killed him, and Coyote
had to run some more. Rock chased him.

He spied another hill and made for it. Rock was close to
him now and Coyote was tired. He saw a hawk and asked for
his help. Hawk said, "All right, get behind me and I will see
what I can do." Coyote got behind Hawk. Hawk flew straight
up in the air and left Coyote sitting there, with Rock coming
right at him. Hawk dropped straight down, hit Rock with his
chest, and smashed it to pieces. Coyote ran and called, "You
will be called 'rock.' You will be able to run downhill but not
uphill. Old women will grind seeds on you. That is what you
will be used for."

He continued his journey. He heard a drum. First he
thought it was in front of him and he would go on, then it
would sound behind him and he would turn around and go
back. He wondered who was beating the drum. He heard

some people singing. When he looked around, he saw elk horns. He thought the sound came from them. There was a hole in the back of the elk head and he peeked in. He saw many people, all painted yellow. They were singing, dancing, and beating the drum. He said, "Oh, my brothers, help me open this. I have good songs, Sun Dance songs." They were dancing the Sun Dance. They let Coyote in. He said, "I will preach." The whistles started and Coyote preached to the dancers and encouraged them to dance.

Then he sat down and started singing. He went to the drum. He shut his eyes and sang. The people thought him queer. They did not trust him. They said, "When he sings he shuts his eyes." When he sang again, they all ran away. The dancers went first, then the others left. When Coyote opened his eyes he was alone. The people who had been in there were Field Mice.

Coyote could not get the elk head off his head, so he said, "I always wanted to be an elk." He went on his journey with the elk head over his head. He thought, "Won't I be glad when the people see me and say, 'Here comes Bull Elk.'" When the people saw him they started shooting at him. He got to the edge of a lake and dropped, he was so very tired. The elk head stuck out of the water, the rest of his body was immersed. The people shouted, "Somebody hit him."

While Coyote was lying there, the people came and admired those great horns. They thought what a huge elk it must be to have such large horns. They wondered how they would get this huge animal out of the water. They said, "We will crack the skull in half and then we can get a better hold on it." Somebody said, "Get an ax." Coyote then heard someone say, "Here is the ax." They started taking the meat off the head. Someone said, "Hit it with the ax right here between the horns." They cracked the head open, pried it apart, and Coyote leaped out and ran. They all cried, "Coyote!"

Coyote went on to the river. On the sandy banks were some long-legged birds. He teased them and then said,

"Brothers, I always wanted to be a bird like you. Put some feathers on me." They said, "Oh, no. We cannot trust you." Coyote said, "I always wanted to be a bird like you. I can make a noise just like you do." They said, "Let us hear you." Then they made their noise and Coyote imitated it. They made him wings. They told him that they got their food from under the water and used their long bills to get it. Coyote hunted under the water too. They said, "There is a fine lake over there. We fly right over the camps to reach the lake. The children in camp always look up at us and cry out, 'That one is mine, that one is mine.' They all like us and want to claim us, especially the leader." Coyote said, "When we get to the camps I will be the leader. Let me fly first." They agreed but told him not to look down on the children but to look straight ahead.

When they got near the camp Coyote went ahead, making a noise like the rest of the birds. The children were all crying, "Mine, mine." It sounded pleasing to Coyote. They flew around and around the lake and then settled down on the bank. They went in the water and got something to eat. Coyote went with them, sticking his nose in the water.

Finally Coyote wanted to fly over the camps again and he said, "I do like to hear the children claiming us." They returned. Coyote said, "We will go in two lines with a space between us." They flew over the camps. The children were calling, "Mine. I claim him." Just as they got over the camps Coyote looked down and he fell down into the middle of the camps. The birds said, "Where is our leader?" and then they saw him on the ground. He lay there and he heard someone talking.

A man said to his wife, "Get the bird. He is good to eat." Coyote lay there and watched the woman come to him. When she touched him, he jerked. The woman was frightened, for she had thought him dead. She ran back and her husband said, "Where is the bird?" She said, "He frightened me." The man said, "He is dead." He told another woman to get the bird. He said, "Don't be frightened. He is good to eat." Another woman tried to grab Coyote and he jumped. She was frightened and ran back to camp. The man said, "Where is the bird?" and the woman replied, "He frightened me," and the man said, "He is dead." The man then said, "Bring me my bow and arrows." Coyote saw the man coming with his bow and arrows. Just as the man got near, Coyote jumped up and the man cried, "Coyote!" and everyone came running to see Coyote.

Coyote returned to the lake. He wanted the birds to give him more feathers. He said, "If you will give me some more feathers, I will tell you something I saw." They would not trust him. They flew away. Coyote sat on the bank and made fun of them. He said they had funny long legs and that they were ugly.

When he was rested he went on down the creek. He heard somebody talking and laughing. The people were tossing something up in the air. Coyote watched them and said, "What are you laughing at?" The people were Chickadees. They were eating *yampa*. They said, "We take out our eyes and throw them up in the air. It makes us laugh and the eyes make a funny noise when they come back in our heads." Coyote said he would like to do it, too, so they fixed his eyes so he could. They spoke a certain word when they threw up their eyes and the *yampa* fell in their hands. Then they spoke the word again and their eyes came back. Coyote liked the *yampa* and he liked the way his eyes felt when they had been up in the air.

Coyote accompanied them for a way and then he said, "I am tired. I will go my way and you go yours." They told him never to throw his eyes up when he was in a grove of yellow willows. Coyote kept on throwing up his eyes and enjoyed doing it. He went to a grove of yellow willows and said, "I don't believe what they said." He threw up his eyes and called the magic word, but his eyes did not return. Everything was dark. He called and called but his eyes did not come back.

Now he had to find his way by scenting. He could not

see. He kept on his way. He heard some laughter. By scent he decided it was two women. One had a little bell. The women came to him. He kept his back turned to them. He asked what kind of women they were and they told him they were Cinnamon Bear girls. Coyote said, "Why that is the kind of bear I am. Why don't we all go together. I will be your husband and take care of you." So they all went on together.

The girls saw some buffalo and said, "You better kill a buffalo so we can have some meat to eat." Coyote did not know what to do, but he said, "All right, I have my bow and arrows." They said, "Go this way and sneak up on them." Coyote went the wrong way. He could not see where they had pointed. The girls wondered what was the matter with him. Poor Coyote shot anywhere and the buffalo ran away. The girls said, "When are you going to gather up your arrows?" and Coyote replied, "I have two women here to do that for me." They told him he had killed one buffalo and asked him to butcher it. Coyote said, "I killed it, you women can butcher." They said, "No, we have to make a shade," but Coyote told them to butcher and said he would make the shade.

The women butchered and then came to Coyote. They said, "Why did you leave so many holes in the shade?" He replied, "If our enemies come from the north we can escape by that hole, and if they come from the south we can go out that hole. No matter which way they come we can escape easily."

They had a feast. While they were eating, Coyote would not look straight at them. The older girl said, "We better look in your head for lice. Put your head in my lap." He lay down with his face on her lap and told them to look in the back of his head. He put his feet on the lap of the other girl. The girl at his head wished that Coyote would go to sleep. The one at his feet said, "What is the matter with his face?" Coyote went to sleep and they turned his head and saw that he had no eyes, just round, red holes. The girl at his feet got a log and put his feet on it and the other girl put a log under his head. They ran away.

Uintas, White Rocks, 1909. Edward Sapir. Marriott Library Special Collections.

Coyote woke up and thought that his head was lying on something hard. He discovered his head and feet were lying on logs. He wondered where the women had gone. He sniffed around, picked up their scent and followed them. They looked back and saw him coming. They went up a rocky cliff. Coyote almost caught up to them. The girls said, "We will stand behind this rock and when he comes we will throw the bell down the cliff." They were right at the edge of the cliff. They threw the bell down the cliff and Coyote leaped after the sound. He fell down and down. He broke his leg and he cried, for it hurt. He sat there and took a stick and poked it in his leg and removed the marrow, which he ate. The women saw him doing this and cried, "There is someone eating the marrow from his own leg." Coyote called back, "I am eating the mountain goat I killed."

The girls ran away. Blue Jay came flying by and Coyote asked him to fix his leg. He did. Then Coyote went to his brother's house. When his brother saw that Coyote was blind, he killed a mountain goat and took its eyes and put them in Coyote's head.

—ARCHUP

(Stella LaRose, translator)

Bear Elopes with Mountain Lion's Wife

Bear was singing at the Bear Dance. A woman and her daughter were sitting nearby. The girl got up and started to dance. She took Bear for a partner and got under his blanket with him. Then they went away together. She was going to be his wife. It was Mountain Lion's wife who went away with Bear. Next morning Mountain Lion followed them. They were up on a hill. The woman said, "My husband is dangerous. If he sees us, he will kill us." Bear boasted, "I am strong myself." He went to a tree and pulled it up to show how strong he was. The woman said, "My husband picks up big boulders and throws them."

Mountain Lion went around the hill and got in front of them. He hid there and waited for them to come by. Bear pulled up another bush to show how strong he was. The woman kept saying that she knew her husband would kill them. Bear came up and Mountain Lion got behind him, grabbed him around the waist, tossed him up in the air, and threw him down. He broke his back in two. Then Mountain Lion took his wife again.

While Bear had been with the woman, she wanted to know when he was going to have intercourse with her. He refused her, saying he only had sexual relations in spring and summer. She kept coaxing him. Mountain Lion did not punish his wife when he got her back, for she told him she had not had intercourse with Bear.

—ARCHUP

(Stella LaRose, translator)

Bear and Fly

Bear and Fly had a quarrel. Bear said to Fly, "You go to people's places and you spoil their food. You lay eggs in their food." "Oh," said fly, "I only put salt on their food. You do worse than that. You disfigure the faces of humans. You scratch them all up. I don't do that."

—ARROCHIS
(Stella LaRose, translator)

Porcupine's Adventures

Porcupine left his children and went on a journey. He told his children to stay at home. He said he was going east to where the sun rose. Porcupine was going to visit other tribes. He wanted to go where there was fighting. He wanted excitement. He left his wife and children at home. They used to say, "My father is coming home with many scalps." Porcupine's wife said to her children, "I am afraid you may have no father now. Perhaps he has been killed. I know he went away and left us." Every morning the children would say, "Father will come today with many scalps," and their mother would say, "I am afraid he has been killed." When he had been gone for a long time, the children would talk about their father all day.

One day they were looking out and they noticed a certain hill and said, "I believe Father is over that hill. See that dark spot over there that looks like a cedar tree? I believe that is the bunch of scalps he is bringing back." Sure enough, it was scalps strung on a spear. Half the length of the spear was loaded with scalps. So Porcupine came home. The woman said, "The children have been saying you would bring back some scalps." "See that dark spot over there that looks like a tree? That is the scalps." So Porcupine took white clay and painted his children's faces with his hands. When they got there they circled around the spear that had scalps on it. They skipped around, singing. That is how Porcupine brought home scalps for his children to dance around.

Then Porcupine wanted to go toward the sunset to fight. The wife and children stayed home while he went on his journey. Porcupine saw some buffalo tracks and they led toward the water. The buffalo had just crossed when Porcupine got there. He sat on the bank and watched. He called them. He thought he would make one of them come and get him. He called, "One of you come over and get your aunt." A buffalo said, "There is our aunt, we will have to get her across the river." They said, "Which one of us do you want to come and get you, this one?" "No," said Porcupine. The next buffalo said, "Who, me?" Porcupine said, "No."

So it kept on until the last and best-looking buffalo called and Porcupine said, "You come." That buffalo swam over and said, "Where are you going to ride, on my head?" "No, I am afraid that I would fall off if you shook your head. I would fall off if I were on your back. That is dangerous. I am afraid that if I ride on your tail I would fall off if you switched your tail." "There is only one place where you would be safe," the buffalo said. "Crawl in my rectum." "No, I am afraid that you might want to defecate and I would fall out. Porcupine wanted to crawl up the buffalo's penis, and he did. Away they went. Buffalo said, "When we get near the edge of the river you will hear me go over the rocks. Then you will know we are almost there."

While the Porcupine was sitting in there he injured the buffalo with his quills. He tore up his lungs and his heart and his liver. Just as they got to the bank the buffalo fell dead. When he fell, Porcupine crawled out. He walked around examining the buffalo. He had no knife with which to butcher. When he discovered this, he cried out, "What am I going to butcher with?" While he was saying this, Coyote appeared. "Here is my knife. Butcher with this." "What did you hear me say?" said Porcupine. Coyote said, "I heard you say, 'What will I butcher with?'" "I was not saying that," said Porcupine. "I was saying that I wondered what I was going to make my arrows with." They argued over what Porcupine had said.

After Coyote had looked around he discovered the buffalo. It was the fattest he had ever seen. Then he said, "We will jump over the buffalo and the one that makes the best jump will butcher." Porcupine had to agree, though he knew he could not jump. Porcupine ran and jumped but he landed right on top of the buffalo. Coyote jumped over it. Porcupine said, "My moccasins made me slip. I will take them off." So Porcupine tried barefooted. He jumped again. Coyote wished that he would miss and he wished so hard that Porcupine jumped on the buffalo. Coyote jumped clear over. Porcupine said, "I think it was my leggings that bothered me." He tried jumping without his leggings, but again he landed on the buffalo. Porcupine sat there and watched Coyote butcher.

After Coyote finished butchering, he cut out the entrails and told Porcupine to take them and feed the little water bugs. He gave the empty entrails to Porcupine. Coyote asked, "Did you feed the bugs the entrails that had nothing in them and did you keep the full entrails?" Porcupine said, "No." Coyote asked the bugs if Porcupine had given them the best parts and they said, "No." Coyote said to Porcupine, "You lied to me." He beat him and left him lying as if dead.

Coyote piled up the meat. He thought he had killed Porcupine. He defecated beside the pile of meat. When he started off he thought he heard something speak. It was the feces that he had left to watch Porcupine. Every time Porcupine moved, the feces called to Coyote. Coyote heard, but he thought Porcupine could not get up. But Porcupine did get up and hit the feces with his tail and broke them.

Coyote went to his home and told his family he had a lot of meat, both porcupine and buffalo. One daughter wanted to make her youngest brother a pair of quilled moccasins. Another said she would make a pair for her mother. Another said, "I will make my father a pair." They went to get the meat. Coyote told his daughters to go ahead, and he stayed

Near White Rocks, 1909. Edward Sapir. Marriott Library Special Collections.

behind with his wife. The children went on and Coyote copulated with his wife on the way. The children would call back, "Which way?" and Coyote would answer, "That way." He continued to have intercourse with the woman. This kept up all day. Finally the girls cried, "Where?" and Coyote called, "Right over there."

While he was coming along, wasting his time, Porcupine got up after destroying the feces. He sat on the meat and called, "Pine tree grow, pine tree grow." The pine tree heard him and it grew up. It rose up with Porcupine and the meat on it.

Coyote and his family could not find the meat. They searched. Porcupine sat up there on the tree and thought, "I wish that youngest pot-bellied boy would look up." He did and said, "Oh, there it is, way up there." Coyote looked up and said, "My friend, throw me down some meat." Porcupine said, "No." Coyote begged and begged and Porcupine finally said, "I will give you some meat if you will all lie down under the tree." They obeyed. Porcupine thought he would throw down the ribs and kill them. He wished they would all die except the youngest pot-bellied boy. So they were all killed except this child, who jumped away. Porcupine called to him and said, "Climb up here," but the child could not, for he did not know how to climb. Porcupine told him to do it and finally he managed it.

Porcupine gave him meat and he ate until he could hold no more. He told Porcupine that he wanted to defecate and asked where he should go. Porcupine said, "I go sit on a branch over there." The child went to a branch and said, "Right here?" Porcupine said, "No, go a little farther." "Here?" "No, go a little farther." The Porcupine kept telling him to go farther until the child was on the very end of the branch. Porcupine said, "There." Porcupine shook the tree and the child fell and his paunch popped like a blowout.

There is a big pine some place in Nevada. They take care of that old tree because that is the pine tree that grew up with Porcupine and the meat on it.

—ARCHUP
(Stella LaRose, translator)

Council on the Seasons

Coyote used to pile beaver hides. All the different kinds of birds were interested in what they were going to do about the winter months. They used to go to Coyote's place and count the hides. They would go there and see what they could hear. There was one man who never used to laugh. Everybody noticed that he never laughed. They said, "I wonder why that man never laughs." A number of them talked together and said, "We will tell him to gather some pine gum." The man went.

While he was gone, they wondered what they could do to make him laugh. They said, "When we say funny things and enjoy ourselves, he never laughs with us." Magpie said,

"I know how to make him laugh. I could do something funny to make him laugh." Magpie painted himself with white paint. When the man came back with the pine gum, Coyote called all the people and told them to get ready to count the hides again. The man who had never laughed was Bald Eagle. While they were all there Magpie came to the door. He started dancing. His big stomach bounced around. Bald Eagle laughed until his stomach shook too. He shouted with laughter. They said, "His breath smells very bad. No wonder he never laughed."

Morning came. In the evening Coyote went to gather some gum. While he was gone the rest of the animals and birds got together and talked about the winter. They said, "We are afraid that Coyote will make the winter too long and we will not be able to get anything to eat and we will all starve to death before spring." They searched for one of the birds who had only three toes. They chose Sage Hen. Then they chose another one, Hawk. Hawk said, "Yes, I am a bird with only three toes." That was what they discussed while Coyote was getting gum.

Owl sat outside all the time, watching for dawn. Then Owl was to signal and they were all to rush out and break up the council. They told Rattlesnake to crawl under the rocks. That night, when everything was all planned, Coyote returned and said, "It looks as though you people have been talking about something." Owl made a noise outside and that warned Coyote.

Hawk was restless. He kept moving around. Coyote said, "What have you to say? You are restless. You won't sit still. Is there something you have to say?" While they were still in council, Owl made a noise outside and told the birds to get ready to jump out of there. Coyote said, "Don't say that." Hawk burst out then and said, "Three toes." They all got up and ran in all directions. Hawk ran into thick brush and Coyote chased him. Hawk threw his eyes at the bushes and they caught there and turned into wild currants. The bushes were loaded with currants.

Coyote said when he got there that what they counted

was twelve hides and there would be that many months in the
year. The winter months were to be three, the number of
Hawk's toes. Then Coyote added the "buckskin end." [That
is the time when the people will be hungry at the end of three
months of winter and they will eat rawhide *parfleches* and
other rawhide articles because all their food will be gone
then.]

When they were counting hides, what they did was to
pull a hair out of the hide and each hair meant a month of winter. They were afraid winter would never end. There are still
big piles of ashes at the place where they used to council.

—ATWINE
(Stella LaRose, translator)

Mosquito

Mosquito was a tall man. He carried two big sacks on his
back. A man went hunting in the mountains. Mosquito went
to this man and said to him, "I have all kinds of things in my
sack, paint and other things you like. I want you to go home
and tell your people to come to this certain place. It is a shel-
tered place in the mountains where the wind doesn't blow."
The man went to tell his people. Then they all went to that
place. Men, women, and children went. They were all waiting there and Mosquito came. He sat down among them and
unfastened his sacks. The sacks were full of mosquitoes and
they bit all the people and killed them. Since then we have
had mosquitoes.

One man had been away hunting and didn't know about
the meeting in the mountains. When he returned home he
found no one there. The camps were empty. He set out to
search and finally he found all his people, dead. He went to
another group of people and told them how he had found all
his people dead. He said he did not know what had caused it.

Mosquito met another man in the mountains and told him
just what he had told the first man—to tell his people to come

to a certain place in the hills. When this man returned to his camp, he delivered the message. The people had just heard from the stranger how he had found his people dead, and they guessed that Mosquito might have been responsible. The chief said, "We will go there all right. First, you men get a big tree and whittle the end of it. Meanwhile the rest of us will go there. We will wait for Mosquito, but we will not give him a chance to do anything. One of you men will lie down and put your head on his sacks and we will see what Mosquito says. Hide your clubs."

Mosquito came. Two men lay on his sacks. Mosquito said, "Don't do that. You will break something in there." They grabbed Mosquito and beat him with their clubs until he died. They did not open the sacks. They did not know what to do with Mosquito. Someone said, "Get big piles of sagebrush and put Mosquito on them and burn him." They did this and they put the two sacks on the fire also. They burned Mosquito and his two sacks. The mosquitoes we have now are those that escaped from that fire. They were dangerous and would eat you up and kill you.

—ATWINE

(Stella LaRose, translator)

Frog and Toad

There was Frog and there was Toad. Toad said to his brother, "Let us go see the people. We will go on a long journey." They sharpened their knives. They traveled on and on and finally they came to a big hill. They thought they would go to the top and see how far it was to the camps. When they were on top they could see some tents. Toad said, "We will rest here until midnight and then we will go down to the camps." They decided that when they got down there they would be sure to go to the chief's tent. It would have yellow around the bottom.

When they traveled on, Toad, the older brother, would just jump once and then let a long time elapse before he jumped again. Frog said, "Is that the way you are going to go when they see us and we try to escape? They will chase us." Frog could go faster than Toad.

When they thought it was midnight they left their hill and went down to the camps. Everyone had gone to bed. They went straight to the chief's tent. They hopped to the doorway side by side. They kept on hopping and got to the chief, who was sleeping with his two wives. They hopped until they got on his chest. They pulled the blanket off his face. They had their knives with them and they cut his head off. Then they scalped him. Then they hid under the pillows.

In the morning the women got up and got breakfast all ready and did not look at their husband. Then they said, "You better get up and eat now. Everything is ready." The man did not move. They rushed up and took off the blanket and there he was with his head cut off. They began to cry and went outside and told the rest of the people, "Our chief has been killed!"

They hunted around to see who had killed him. They could not see tracks anywhere. They wanted to move camp. They got a forked tree to carry the dead man. The women got their things all packed up. When they cleaned up the brush they had slept on, the women moved the part of the brush that had served as a pillow and there were the two brothers, Frog and Toad.

These two had been at that game a long time. They had killed many people in that way, but always before they had escaped. The brothers still had the man's scalp. The women cried, "Here are those who killed the chief." The people chased them. Toad was very slow. Frog could go faster than Toad and he beat him to the spring. The people killed Toad, who still had the scalp in his hand. They caught him because he was so slow. They saw Frog, but he got to the spring and clawed his way through the mud. The pursuers were so angry they fought among themselves.

—ATWINE

(Stella LaRose, translator)

Theft of Fire

There was a bird family. They had no matches. Coyote got all
the birds together. He wanted to ask them something. He
saw a spark fly from the west, and he wanted to know where
that fire came from. He said, "I would like one of you birds to
go clear up to where the sky is fastened." The sky was
braced by poles, and Coyote wanted the bird to go up there
where the sky was fastened and see where that spark came
from.

He sent a small bird. The little bird flew but he could not
get there. He was a little bird that lives in the desert. He
came back. Then Coyote sent Magpie. He flew a little farther
than the first, but then he fell. The third bird was Crow. He
flew a little farther than Magpie, but then he dropped to the
ground. Coyote had all the different birds there together, so
he could send any of them. The fourth bird he sent up was
Eagle. Eagle flew the farthest yet, but he could not make it
and returned to earth. Then Coyote called on Hummingbird.
He flew up. They could not see him. He disappeared. Hummingbird got there and sat up there on that pole and watched
the fire.

Coyote was frightened. He said that Hummingbird had
been gone a long time. "I am worried about him. I am afraid
that he has gone so far he has lost his breath." Hummingbird
saw all he could and then he returned. "I saw what you
wanted to discover. There is a great, big fire, far away.
There are cattails on fire." "Yes," said Coyote, "that is what
I wanted you to find out." Coyote wanted them all to go to
the place where the fire was. The people who had the fire
were blackbirds. Coyote wanted the birds to go with him and
play Hand Game against the blackbirds. That is why blackbirds sit around in cattail patches.

They went on this journey. It took them a long time to
get there, but they finally arrived. Coyote challenged the
blackbirds to a Hand Game. Coyote said, "I want no bets but
fire. You use fire for your bet and I will put up my stakes."

Coyote was all dressed up. He had some pine gum on his hair. They started the game. Coyote was getting the best of the game. The blackbirds had only one stick left. Coyote ran and got the fire. The gum in his hair caught fire. That was why he had put it there. Then he ran away and the blackbirds ran after him.

Camp Robber was the bird next to Coyote. The blackbirds were catching up with them. When Coyote tired, Camp Robber took the fire and ran. When he grew tired, another bird took it. Magpie took the fire and carried it. Coyote had come along while Camp Robber had it and he grew angry and hit Camp Robber. He broke his leg. When he discovered what he had done, he put a piece of straw on it and tied it up. "Oh, I broke my friend's leg." Then Coyote went on with the rest of the birds.

The blackbirds gained on Magpie. Hummingbird then took the fire and he went so fast they could not see him. He ran so fast the fire almost went out. Hummingbird left them all behind and the blackbirds gave up and went home. They said, "We will let them go." They were very angry and said many things about Coyote. "Winter will come and he will die. There will be a flood and he will be washed away." They made many bad wishes for Coyote.

They wondered which bird should be responsible for fire, now that they had it. They asked Jackrabbit if he would take care of it. It started to rain and storm and they asked him, "Can you sit and endure this?" "Yes," said Jackrabbit. "I will put the fire under me and I will sit over it. I will take care of that fire and protect it." Afterward, Coyote went to Jackrabbit and asked him if he still had the fire. Jackrabbit said he still had it. Coyote said, "Well, we better make a fire now. I will go over here."

He went to the cliff and started making a noise such as mice make. Wood Rat stuck his head out and Coyote said, "Throw me out some bark, my friend." Wood Rat threw out some bark. Coyote made his fire with that bark. "Well," he said, "I have my fire made now and I think I will go back and kill Wood Rat." He went to the cliff and made a noise like a mouse. Wood Rat stuck his head out and Coyote shot him with his bow and arrow and killed him.

There was fresh snow. Jackrabbit made a lot of fresh tracks. He ran back and forth. He made Coyote think there were many rabbits there instead of just one rabbit. They all rushed out to go rabbit hunting. Then Coyote saw that one Jackrabbit and started shooting with his bow and arrow. Every time he shot an arrow, Jackrabbit would blow and make that arrow fly in a different direction. After a while Jackrabbit got tired of having Coyote shoot at him. He thought, "I will let him shoot me in the ears and then I will run back into my hole." Coyote shot him in the ears and Jackrabbit ran into his hole and took the arrow with him. So Coyote did not get the rabbit.

Everyone had fire then. All the birds and animals had fire.

—ATWINE

(Stella LaRose, translator)

Coyote Learns to Fly

Coyote was traveling beside the river. He saw some people beside the river. It was a flock of geese. He said, "I would like to be like you birds. I would like all of you to give me some feathers." The geese said, "You might get us in trouble. You might get to calling before we do and you would get us into trouble." "No, I will not do that," said Coyote, and he coaxed for some feathers. He got all covered with feathers.

"Ngah, ngah," he said, "that is the kind of noise I will make." He practiced lifting himself up. They said, "We always do this way when we start to fly. And we go along the edge of the water and stick our bills down in the mud. That is the way we eat." They illustrated and Coyote imitated them.

They said, "We have another place where we eat, a big

"Coyote" dance, White Rocks, 1909. Edward Sapir. Marriott Library Special Collections.

lake. We always return to this place. There are many camps below here and we fly in two rows high over those tents and the little boys all come out and call, 'That leader is mine, the next one is mine.' They all keep on claiming us, but we never look down." Coyote said, "I want to be your leader when you fly over those camps."

They started to fly. The geese flew first and Coyote was the last to take off. When they got high up in the air, Coyote said, "Let me take the lead." They let him go ahead. The children came out and called, "I'll take the leader!"

They went over to the big lake. "We don't land right away," they said. "We go round and round and get lower and lower and finally we light." Coyote said, "I liked having the children claiming us." Coyote imitated the way they ate. His nose was stuck in the mud and water.

Coyote said, "I think we had better go back. This time we will go in a double row." (They had gone single-file the first time.) They made a noise just before they set off and then they flew back the way they had come. When they neared the camps they formed a double-file. Coyote was in the lead. The boys looked and saw them and started calling. Coyote wondered, "They never look down. I wonder about that. I am going to look down." When they were right over the tents, he looked down and he started falling right down and the boys cried, "What is the matter with the leader, he is falling!"

He fell and lay there listening to the talking in the tent. "Go and get him, he is good to eat. Let's not waste him." A woman came to pick him up, but when she touched him he moved and she was frightened and would not pick him up. She returned to the tipi. Another woman came out and the same thing happened. Then an old man said, "Give me my bow and arrows. I will kill him." Coyote heard this. When the old man drew near, he jumped up and ran. The man cried, "Coyote! It is just an old Coyote!"

Then Coyote returned to where he had met the geese. "Brothers, I want to be one of the birds again. I liked it." "Oh, no," they said, "you do not obey orders." Coyote said, "I will tell you all about it if you will let me be a bird again." "No, you do not listen to us. You can stay Coyote." Coyote grew angry and said, "I don't want to be one of you. Your bill is ugly, your tail is ugly, and you are ugly birds." The geese said, "We do not listen to you," and they went away.

—ARCHUP
(Stella LaRose, translator)

Coyote Becomes a Mother

Coyote gathered together a number of pregnant women. He wanted to adopt a child. He laid the women down and operated on them. He found four girl babies and one boy. When he had found the boy he operated on himself and made himself into a woman. He then inserted the infant's penis into himself. Then he tied a rag on his hair, took a stick in his hand, and he was a pregnant woman. He got bark to make a bed. He was preparing to become a mother. He began to have pains. The infant was born. Then, as the women do, he took some of the bark and wiped his face. He scratched his head with a stick. He went out and ran. He dug a pit in the ground and put hot rocks in it as women do.

Everyone was curious to see Coyote's baby. All the animals came and said, "What a lovely baby you have." The burros came last. All the animals were pleased to see Coyote's baby. They all wanted to be like him and have babies. The mule kicked and said he did not want to have a baby. That is why mules never give birth.

—ARCHUP

(Stella LaRose, translator)

Bat

Coyote lived beside Bat. Bat was cooking seeds. Coyote said to his little boy, "Go see what Bat is doing." When the boy went in, Bat was just taking the food out of his pot and he said, "Hold out your hands and I will give you some." Bat put the hot stuff in the boy's hand and burned it.

Coyote had a wife, two daughters, and the little boy. He told his daughter to go see Bat. Bat was eating dinner when she went in. The girl sat down. Bat continued eating and did not look up. The girl jumped up and went home. Coyote said, "What is he doing now?" The girl answered, "Just eating." Coyote then sent the other daughter to see what Bat was doing. Coyote thought Bat might want to marry one of the girls. The second daughter went and returned. Coyote said, "What is he doing now?" "He has finished eating." "What did he say?" "He never spoke to me."

Then Coyote went to Bat. "I am discouraged," he said. "I have been trying to get some mountain sheep, but I can't get any. I would like to have someone go with me. You go with me. We will go in this direction." They went hunting together.

Coyote said, "Bat, you go first. Take these women with you and show them where you gathered your seeds. I will go this way. I will call out every once in a while." Bat took the two women and showed them where he gathered his seeds. After he left the women there, he went on to where Coyote had told him to station himself. Coyote said the mountain sheep would come by there. He sat and waited for Coyote.

He watched the women while he sat there. One of the daughters strayed away from the others. Bat followed her and had intercourse with her. Then he went back and waited for the mountain sheep. The other girl strayed away and Bat followed her and had intercourse. He could hear Coyote calling, so he returned to the spot where he was stationed. Then he saw Coyote's wife stray off and he followed her and had intercourse with her.

Bat returned to his station. Coyote came along with a band of mountain sheep. He called, "They are going right by you." The leader was not far from Bat, and behind the leader were many mountain sheep. Coyote was quite far behind.

Bat hid behind the rocks. Coyote was calling, "They are going just where I told you they would go. Where are you?" Bat hid under the rock and the mountain sheep were jumping over him. Bat came out from under the rock and shot the last mountain sheep, an old female. When he shot her the whole band of sheep fell dead.

Coyote said, "Where are they? I saw them all going over this way. Where were you?" Bat showed him the last one that had been shot and the others that had all fallen dead. Coyote was surprised to see all the sheep dead. They decided to butcher. Coyote said, "You butcher this one and I will butcher that one." The one that Bat was butchering was fat, and Coyote's was not. Coyote said, "How is your sheep?" Bat replied, "Nice and fat." Then Coyote said, "I will take that one and you butcher this one."

Every time Bat started to butcher one of the sheep, Coyote came and said, "I told you to butcher this one." He did this every time Bat started to butcher. Coyote took all the fat ones and left Bat just the last old female that he had shot. Bat took all the poor ones home with him. Coyote got his two daughters and his wife and they each took a load of the good, fat meat to their camp. This hurt Bat's feelings. He left his camp beside Coyote and went away. That was the end. He left.

—ARCHUP
(Stella LaRose, translator)

The Dog Whose Wife Left Him

Dogs used to marry each other. One dog had a wife. Another dog came and took her away and the dogs fought. A group of dogs would attack the one who had the female and beat him till his bones were broken. When Dog discovered his wife was gone, his mother urged him not to do anything. She said, "Your wife is gone. Her family are mean people. They might hurt you." But that evening Dog saw his wife, grinding. She was fixing food for her new husband. He sat in the doorway where she was grinding. He reached out his hand and took a little of what she ground. She hit his hand and pushed it away. Her new husband was lying nearby. Dog got mad and pushed the woman. That aroused her new husband and he got up and said, "We will fight you." The other dogs joined him and they beat the deserted husband. Poor Dog went home to bed.

Next morning his mother woke him and told him to get up. He went outside to defecate and then went back to bed and covered his head. His mother called him to come to breakfast and wondered why he didn't move when she called him. She pulled the blankets away from him and found that he was dead. She said, "I told you not to go over there. I knew they would treat you as they did." When she went outside she saw where Dog had defecated and she saw that he had defecated his bones.

—ARCHUP
(Stella LaRose, translator)

Crow and His Wife, Dog

Crow married one of the dog women and took her to his home. She was a beautiful woman. Crow said, "I am a good hunter. You will not starve." He went hunting every day, but he never brought home any game. He would say, "I could find nothing but dry stuff." He never brought her anything to eat. She was starving. Her beautiful hair got all stiff and matted. Crow used to say, "Just dry stuff. That is why I could find nothing."

One of the woman's brothers said, "I think I will visit my brother-in-law." His mother said, "You better take this meat with you." He took the meat with him. When he got to Crow's place, there sat his sister with a big head. She said, "I have no food to give you. I am starving. I have nothing to eat." Her brother said, "I have some food with me."

They ate what he had brought. Crow came home while his brother-in-law was there and said, "I believe I will go and get some fresh meat." But when he came back in the evening, he brought nothing with him. Next morning, he said the same thing, "I think I will go get some fresh meat." His wife said, "That is what he says all the time, but he never brings anything." Her brother said, "Why don't you come home with me?" She left and went back to her mother's house.

When Crow returned that night he found no one at home. He followed the tracks and came to the dogs' house. He went looking for his wife. Her mother hid her. Crow had a moustache. He looked in the camp of his wife's family and said, "I know she is here." The mother said, "No, I have not seen her." "Hurry up and bring her out," said Crow. He stood in the door. He urged the woman to make her daughter come out. "Someone's anger is growing," he said. This was his way of telling the woman he was angry. "Hurry up, bring her out. There is a bad feeling getting near." Crow had his bow and arrows with him. "Now," said Crow, "it *is* here."

He went into the tent and jerked his wife out from under the blankets. He kicked her and stamped on her. He beat her to death. The other dogs just sat and looked on. They were afraid of Crow because he had whiskers. Then Crow went away. Everywhere he went people said, "There goes Crow. He is dangerous. He killed his wife. That is the way Crow does."

—ARCHUP

(Stella LaRose, translator)

Owl Woman and Skunk

Owl was sick. He had stepped on a rabbit bone and hurt his foot. He died. He told his little boy to take his mother to the Hawk. "He is the one to feed you good," he said. So the mother and the little boy went on their journey. They came to Skunk's house. Only Old Lady Skunk was there. When Mr. Skunk came home he said, "It looks like somebody has been here and sat right here." She said, "No, that is where I sat." He said, "It's not your size tracks. You go sit down and let me see." She sat where Owl Woman had sat but she didn't fit the tracks. Her husband said, "Where did that person go who was here?" So she had to tell the truth. "Old Owl's wife sat there." He said, "Which way did they go?" She said, "This way."

And he went and took after that woman and he caught up with them and said, "Can I be your husband?" She said, "My husband told me to go to Hawk and be Hawk's wife." Skunk said, "What about me? Have me for a husband." And he kept on coaxing her and coaxing her. After a while she reached in her hair and got a handful of lice and threw them on the hill. She didn't want Skunk. Those lice turned into mountain goats. She said, "There are some goats, let me see you kill them." He said, "All right," and he took off his robe and gave it to her to wear while he killed the goats.

When he got some distance away, Owl Woman and her son ran away and they put Skunk's robe on a wild rosebush. Skunk went and killed a goat and when he came back he

found they were gone. He found his robe. He thought the
woman was under the robe and he grabbed it, but all he got
was this rosebush. They were quite a way off by this time.
They looked back and could see nothing but smoke. Skunk
had farted and they said, "His fart is going to catch up with
us." It came and exploded just like gas and spread all over.
They had to breathe it, and she got so weak she just keeled
over and died. The boy didn't die.

—ARCHUP
(Stella LaRose, translator)

Owl's Widow Seeks a Husband

Badger was asleep at his home, not far from here. He said, "I
have had a dream, a very dangerous dream." He said to his
mother, "Look all around. Perhaps you will see something
strange." His mother went up on a hill. She could see a little
spot far away on the flats. She could not see what it was. She
returned and told her son what she had seen. She said, "Far
over there I saw something I had never noticed there before,
a little dark spot." "Mother, give me that white clay." Badger
painted his face and got ready to go. He started digging in the
ground, digging his way. He went in the direction of the dark
spot his mother had described. He went underground and
came up right where the woman and her son were lying. He
did not come up in just the right spot, so he went underground again and came up right in the middle of the woman.

He began to doctor the woman. After a while she began
to revive. "I have been asleep a long time," she said. He doctored her again until she felt much better. Then she said, "I
don't know what I will pay you with. I have nothing to give
you for making me well." He said, "Well, give me your
tupugufᵘ." She did not know what he meant. "What is that?"
she said. She guessed everything about herself until she finally got to her vulva. "Is that what you mean?" Badger said,

"Yes." He had intercourse with her and she was completely cured then.

Badger said to her, "When you go on your way, you will hear people making a noise and sounding as though they are having a lot of fun. Don't pay any attention to them. Do not look at them. Stay on your own side and keep on your way." They went on their journey and when they neared the place the boy kept coaxing his mother, "Let's look. Let's peek." "No," she said, "they are dangerous. Badger said not to look." The boy continued coaxing and finally he looked toward the sound. As soon as he looked back, he and his mother began to bleed from the mouth. They both fell to the ground. It was Woodpecker who had been making the noise. Woodpeckers caused bleeding from the mouth.

Badger said to his mother, "I am having a terrible dream." He sent her to look and see if she could see anything. She looked and saw a dark spot way off in the distance. When she returned and told her son she had seen a dark spot, he started and dug his way to that place. He came up from the ground right in front of the woman and the boy. He doctored both of them. They said, "We went to sleep." He said, "I told you not to look that way because I knew this would happen. You disobeyed." After he had doctored, he had to be paid. She knew what he meant now when he asked for her *tupuguf^u*, so she had intercourse with him and paid him. He said, "Keep on your way. I told you where Hawk lived. Do not stop on your way there."

They went to the place where Badger said Hawk lived. There were many camps there. The first tent they came to was occupied by an old woman who said, "I am glad to see you. From which direction did you come?" The woman said, "Owl died, but before his death he told us to come to Hawk. He said Hawk would hunt for us and feed us." The old woman said, "Hawk is not here now. He and many others have gone hunting rabbits."

They waited and finally the men began to come back.

They all had many rabbits. Hawk had not had much luck. He had only one rabbit and that was shot all over. The old woman was Hawk's mother. She had prepared a big fire for the rabbits she thought he would bring home. She had the coals all ready. When he came he had only this one little rabbit, all shot up. She put it in the coals to cook. Hawk said, "I think those rabbits are done. You better dig them out." When she dug out the rabbit it was more meat than they could eat. It had grown and multiplied. They got it out of the coals and started to pull the hair off and prepare for a feast of rabbit.

It grew late. Hawk said, "I think I will go to bed." He flew to the cliffs. The mother said, "My son is a peculiar man. He would frighten you. You would be frightened here." But Owl Woman said, "I am going to go to him." The mother said, "You might catch him there, but you might scare him." Owl told her little boy to stay with the old woman and she went to find her husband-to-be. All the other animals were camped there, including Coyote. Owl Woman followed Hawk to the spot she had seen him go to.

She stared up at the cliffs wondering how she would get up there. She took some of her pubic hair and made a ladder of it that went clear up to Hawk's house in the cliffs. She climbed up on that rope and looked inside a nice stone house. Hawk was asleep there. When she went in and put her hand on him, he woke up frightened and shrieked. Coyote heard and said, "Somebody is after my partner. Perhaps some strangers are after him." When Hawk found it was a woman, he quieted down. Coyote had his scare for nothing. That is the way Hawk married Owl Woman.

Next day everyone knew they were married. Coyote was angry because the woman had not come to his place and married him. He said he was a good hunter and could feed her. He was angry because she had gone to Hawk instead of to him.

—ARCHUP

(Stella LaRose, translator)

Coyote Imitates Mountain Lion

There used to be wild horses when Mountain Lion roamed around. There was a muddy spring. The horses used to go there. Mountain Lion would lie in wait there and kill them when they came to drink. There were some trees by the spring. He would lie in the branches and when the horses went under the tree, Lion would pick out the fattest horse and jump down on him. He would bite him in the back of the neck, then wrap his tail around the animal's neck and drag him to the place where he wanted to eat.

Mountain Lion used to roam all over. One day he saw something and wondered what it was. He went to see and found Coyote bent over an anthill, eating ants. Lion said, "What are you doing?" "I am eating ants." "Don't they sting your mouth?" "No, they do not sting when you get them in your mouth." Lion said, "Come with me, I have a better place to eat than this."

They went to where Lion had cached his meat. Then he told Coyote to go up on a high knoll and see if he could see anything. Coyote said he could see some dust. He watched it. Then he went down the hill and Lion asked, "What did you see?" "I saw a streak of dust, far off." Lion said, "You better go back and see where it is now." So Coyote went back and saw that the dust was closer. He returned to Lion and told him the dust was nearer. Lion told him to go look again and Coyote reported this time that the dust was quite close. Lion sent him back to the hill again. This time the dust was still closer. Lion sent him up again, and again he returned and reported the dust nearer. Lion sent him once more and he reported that it was very close. Then Lion said, "You stay here under this tree. Do not move. I will go where I always go, but don't you move. Keep your eyes on me and watch what I do."

Then Lion climbed a tree and lay on the branch. Coyote watched him. The horses came to the place where Lion was hiding in the tree. They were led by a stallion. They began to lick at the mud. When a big, fat animal got under the tree Lion jumped down on him. All the other horses ran. Lion killed the animal. Then he told Coyote to drag the animal to the place where Lion always took his game. Coyote tried but he could not move the animal. Lion said, "This is the way I do it." He put his tail around the neck of the horse and pulled him. He told Coyote to brush off the tracks he had made in the dirt when he pulled the horse. Coyote did that and then went with Lion to the place where Lion always ate his game. There were many bones there. Lion said, "Go ahead. Start eating." Coyote started on the hindquarters. "This is better than eating ants," he said.

Lion said, "If you don't eat all the meat today, you can come back again and have some more. I am going away. Don't try to imitate what I did because the horses will kill you. Go and drink way below the spring. That is where I drink." The Lion went away and left Coyote still eating. "I will be back again sometime," Lion said.

Coyote ate his fill and then went to get a drink. He came back and ate some more. Then he thought he would go away. While he was on his way he saw something way out on the flats. When he got there he saw another coyote eating ants. He went to him and said, "What are you doing?" "Eating ants," the other coyote replied. "Don't they sting your mouth?" "No, they don't sting my mouth." Coyote then said, "I always have good food. Come with me." The second coyote went with him.

Coyote said, "This is where I always get my food." He took him to the place where he and Lion had eaten. There was still some meat there. The second coyote ate some of the horsemeat. Coyote showed him the place where the horses came to water. Then he told him to go up on the knoll and see if he could see anything. The second coyote went up on the hill and looked. He saw a lot of dust rise up in the air and he came down and reported to Coyote. "What did you see?" "I saw dust." "Go look again and see what you can see." A second, third, fourth, and fifth time the old Coyote sent the other one up to see what he could see. Each time he reported the dust was getting nearer. The sixth time he returned and said that the dust was very close. Again Coyote sent him back and this time he said that the dust was *very* close. Coyote said, "You stay right here. Don't move. I am going over there. Watch, but do not move."

The horses came down the hill with the stallion in the lead. Coyote was lying in the branches of the tree over the spring. When a big horse was directly underneath, Coyote jumped down and lit on his back. The horses all ran away. Coyote hung onto his horse as long as he could, but finally he fell off. As he fell, the horse kicked him in the head and killed him. The other coyote sat and watched and then he went off.

Mountain Lion came back and looked for Coyote. He looked for the horses. He watched until they got close and then he got on his perch and waited for the animals. When the horses got there they did not stay very long. They just came and then started to run. They made a noise as though they were frightened and ran back over the hill. "I wonder what has happened to frighten them. I wonder if Coyote scared these horses," Lion thought.

He found Coyote lying dead where the horse had kicked him. "So he tried to imitate me while I was away." He dragged him away. This is the end.

—ARCHUP
(Stella LaRose, translator)

Water Babies (1)

A man named Moon told Archup that he used to sit on the bank of the White River smoking and dream about water babies all the time. That is why the water babies swam along the river and came.

Moon gave tobacco to Water Baby and he sat and smoked it. When he had finished, Moon said, "There are too many people down this way. You go up the other way. If you go down that way the people might kill you." Water Baby obeyed.

Archup asked the man if this were really true and he said yes, that he used to dream about that little Water Baby all the time.

—ARCHUP
(Stella LaRose, translator)

Water Babies (2)

Sometimes a young man would go to water the horses in the morning. If the water baby is female, the young man goes to sleep on the bank. When he wakes he feels someone lying beside him. He looks and sees a beautiful woman in a green dress lying there. He sleeps with her. After a while she coaxes him to go with her under the water. His family will never see him again because he goes under the water to her people.

—ARCHUP
(Stella LaRose, translator)

Water Babies (3)

There used to be water babies in Green River. A man was looking at the river and he heard crying. It sounded just like a baby. He looked and he saw bubbles in the water and there was Water Baby sitting on the water. He cried like a baby. The man was not afraid and he threw a stick. Water Baby went away. The water kept rising. Then the man dreamed every night. He saw the water coming to get him. He was frightened. He had those dreams because he had thrown the stick at Water Baby. The man got sick.

Water Babies are about the size of a man's hand. They have long, black hair. They cry just like babies.

—PEARL PERIKA
(Mamie Alhandra, translator)

Pearl Perika, 1936. Alden Hayes.

Water Babies (4)

A long time ago a man went to drink water from a river. There was a female water baby there. The man was frightened. Two water babies pulled the man into the river and took him to their home under the water. Their mother told the man that he had to tear the hills down and make them flat. He succeeded in doing it. The two water baby women wanted to marry the man, but he told them they were ugly. They ran away. The old woman followed them and got cactus thorns in her feet walking over the cactus. The cactus had appeared when the girls threw back some of their hair, which turned into cactus. They found the girls on the far side of a hill. They went home with their mother. The man ran away.

Water used to be mean a long time ago. When you tried to get water, the hands of the water people would try to pull you under the water. A man was afraid to draw water. The water baby women cry like babies.

—PEARL PERIKA
(Mamie Alhandra, translator)

Water Babies (5)

A long time ago a group of people camped by a river. They
left a baby in a cradleboard leaned up against a tree near the
river while the women went gathering berries. The baby
woke up and cried. Water Baby came out of the water and
swallowed the baby. Then it crawled into the cradle and cried
just like a baby. It looked like a real baby.

The mother heard the crying and came back to nurse the
child. Water Baby swallowed her breast and the woman cried
out, "Somebody is swallowing me. I don't know what this
baby is. Come and help me." The other women who were
picking berries heard her and came running. They tried to cut
off the breast, but could not do it. Water Baby kept on swallowing until it swallowed the mother.

The women told the husband what had happened to his
wife and his baby. At the same place, later on, he heard a
woman crying and said, "That is my wife crying." He went to
get his wife. He went to the river and was pulled into the water by the Water Babies.

—Pearl Perika
(Stella LaRose, translator)

Water Babies (6)

There used to be water babies in the water down near Ver-
nal. They cried like babies. They were about the size of a
three-year-old child. There was a water baby who lived near
Provo. It cried like a little baby. One boy did not believe the
tales of Water Babies. He wanted to see one. He would not
believe what his family told him. He did not know these Water Babies were bad.

John went fishing with this boy. They saw a Water Baby
nearby, which was drying. The boy wanted to go back and
look at it, but John was frightened and did not want to go.
The Water Babies were on a flat rock. They had long hair.

When the boys came near they dived into the water. The hair floated on top. When the Water Babies went under the water, the water started to rise and the boys ran away.

That is the only time John saw Water Babies.

—JOHN DUNCAN

(Lincoln Picket, translator)

Historical Tale

In the morning Archup woke up early. There was another man lying on the other side of him. When he was lying there something grabbed his big toe and started sucking it. He laid there a long time and that thing moved and went around. And the other man saw that thing, that green thing, and he got up and ran away. And it was that green thing that had been sucking Archup's toe. They finally caught him and chopped him up in little pieces.

Once, when they were going to South Dakota, a water dog got under him. There were three men and his mother. She was making a fire. Archup could feel something licking his penis. He kicked up his legs and said, "Mother, what is touching me?" He threw off his blankets and got up and ran off. His mother wouldn't help him but an old man got a stick and killed it. It was a water dog. There was no water anywhere near for that water dog. He does not know how it got there.

[A water dog is about six inches long with a tail two or three inches long. They have claws like lizards.]

—ARCHUP

(Stella LaRose, translator)

Siants (1)

Sometimes a family would go off by themselves and that is how the enemy could get them and kill them all. Sometimes when they were camped alone, the Siants would come while the man was away hunting and could not protect his family. The witch would scare away the mother and lie down and pretend to be the baby's mother and kill the baby.

—ARCHUP
(Stella LaRose, translator)

Siants (2)

Siants kidnapped a little boy and put him in her basket to carry him home. Once in a while she would sit down to rest. The boy would pick up rocks and put them in the basket with himself. Siants found the basket very heavy. When they went through some brush, the boy reached up, grabbed a cedar limb, and pulled himself out of the basket.

[Pearl described Siants as "an old, wrinkle-faced witch."]

—PEARL PERIKA
(Mamie Alhandra, translator)

Siants (3)

Two men were camping in Colorado. They made camp one night in thick brush. They had gone to sleep when they were awakened by a noise. Siants was sitting by the feet of one of the men. When they saw her they jumped up, got on their horses, and ran away. Later they went back and made a light to see what the Siants looked like, but they did not see her.

[Mamie said her grandmother used to tell stories after the sun went down.]

—PEARL PERIKA
(Mamie Alhandra, translator)

Mamie Alhandra, 1936. Alden Hayes.

Siants (4)

Siants used to camp in the cedars. When the people traveled, Siants would watch them to see where they camped. The people would make a big fire and Siants would know where they were camped. Siants would look for a little boy and then she would try to coax the child away. The father and mother would try to wrestle with her for the boy, but Siants was strong.

Siants would make a fire and would throw the child on the hot coals and roast him and then eat him. Siants would tell the child to get a rock to put under his arm and then she would cook him. When Siants ate a child she ate the flesh and saved the bones. [Informant did not know why the bones were saved, he suggested they might be used to make a little Siants.]

Siants would kidnap children and keep them with her until she was ready to eat them. When the people moved camp, Siants would travel behind them.

There was once a young girl who was sulking in her tent. She sat rubbing her heel in the dirt until she made a hole there. She put her heel in there and braced herself. She looked toward the door and saw it move and there was old Siants. Siants stuck her arm through the door and said, "My son killed a deer but it was a poor one." The girl grabbed that arm and as the girl was well braced with her foot in the hole, she pulled that arm out and threw it on the fire. Siants screamed and ran away. She did not come back.

Siants could not climb a tree. She had rough skin. If you climbed a tree you were safe from Siants.

—ARROCHIS
(Stella LaRose, translator)

Siants (5)

Siants stole a little boy. He was old enough to have some sense. He lived with the Siants family and played with the Siants children. Old Siants called him "Grandson." "Don't cry, Grandson," she would say. The people moved on after Siants had captured the boy. Siants moved on too, and the little boy with her.

When they made camp, Siants went and kidnapped the little boy's sister. When Siants got back to her camp the little girl found her brother there, still alive. This surprised the girl. Siants, said, "Don't cry, my grandchildren." She told them, "Go get a rock to put under your arm and don't cry while you are hunting for it." The children kept on crying. They went quite a distance hunting for the rock. They came to a little ridge, which they followed. On the end of it they saw a little cedar tree. Someone spoke to them from the cedar. It said, "My grandchildren, why are you crying?" They looked and saw a little toad. The girl said, "Siants captured my brother and then she took me. Now we are looking for rocks for Siants. Siants has many children."

There was some sharp stuff on the back of Toad and on

his head. Toad said, "Take some of this stuff and you can kill Siants. Then go home. Keep the stuff and, when you get home, tell your mother to take care of this stuff. She should put it in a fine, clean buckskin bag."

The children went to Siants' camp. Siants realized they had something of which she was frightened. "Throw it away," she said, "you have something there of which I am frightened." Toad had told them to hit Siants with that stuff and kill her. He had said he would come and kill the Siants children. The girl threw the stuff at Siants and killed her. Then Toad came and killed the Siants children. He threw them into the fire. All the Siants family was killed.

Toad said, "Now, my grandchildren, you can go home." They went on the trail and came to where their camp had been located, but no one was there. They went on and on. They kept finding camps that people had left. They picked up scraps of meat and ate them. Then it grew dark and they traveled all night. They met another Siants and she asked, "Where are you going, my grandchildren?" The girl still had the weapon. Siants was reaching for them, but the girl aimed at her and killed her.

Then the children climbed up in an old cedar tree and perched there for the rest of the night. Next morning they went on. They came to another deserted camp. They went on. It grew dark again but they continued. Finally they came to a place where the campfire was still smoking. They went down into a gully, up over the bank, and went on. They came to a hill where there were many pines. They could see campfires burning and they thought they had caught up with their families at last.

They went to their father's camp. Their father said, "Well, my children, how did you escape?" Many people gathered and some of them said, "Perhaps they are not really free. Maybe Siants might be following their trail." The children told how they had escaped. "Some little person gave us this weapon and that is how we escaped." The mother was so happy. She had been sad ever since the children disappeared. She was so happy to have the children back. "I did not know they were still alive." One man got on his horse and rode through camp calling out the news that the children had escaped from Siants.

That stuff from Toad is the only weapon Siants is afraid of. The children told their mother that Toad had said to keep the stuff in a fine, clean, white buckskin. Afterward they had that weapon with which to kill Siants.

Toad had said, "When you children get home, I will come too, but I will be some distance from the people."

—ARROCHIS

(Stella LaRose, translator)

The Man Who Married a Cannibal

A man from one group of people married a woman from another group and went to live with his wife's people. They wanted to go hunting. They said, "We will station our son-in-law on that hill while we chase the game to him." The young man went to his station and sat on a rock on top of the hill. He could hear them shouting every once in a while. While he sat there, a young woman and her child emerged from the timber. The woman said to the boy, "Run. Hurry up. There is danger behind us. Hurry up. There are enemies behind us." The young man let the woman and child go past him. The woman's face was painted. They disappeared into the timber.

Shortly after, he saw a man come out of the timber. He could hear people shouting, "Son-in-law, they are going right for you." When this man got close, he saw that his face was painted. He came near the young man and stopped and looked. He heard his relatives calling, "Son-in-law, they are going straight for you." He wondered what he should do. He took his gun and shot the man who had come out of the timber. He thought, "I have murdered a man." The others then came out of the brush and were shouting, "This is the way they went." The young man sat and watched. They said, "This is the way they went. There are footprints. They must have gone past here. Here he is. Our son-in-law must have killed him. He is lying here dead." They cut the dead man in pieces. The young man sat there. He had murdered that man.

They made a fire near where the dead man lay and started cooking the meat. They laid it in the coals until it was done. The boy never moved from the rock where he was sitting. He just watched them. "Our son-in-law does not want to eat any meat. He is still sitting on the rock." One man said, "You better give him some meat. He is hungry." They took him a piece of meat. He did not eat it. He took it and laid it down. He put it in a crack of the rock. He stuffed it down there and pretended he had eaten it. They had cooked the dead man.

When they finished eating they said, "Let's go home." What they had not cooked, they took home with them. When they got home the women took the rest of the meat and cooked it. The young man did not eat any of it.

He wanted to hunt for game for himself. He killed a mountain sheep and brought it home. His wife saw he had a mountain sheep and she said, "Father, this man has killed one of our horses." The young man said, "I am not like you people who eat human flesh. I have to have this kind of meat."

One day they told the young man and his wife to go look after the horses. He could see no horses. All he saw was manure. His wife said, "They are right here." He said, "Let's make the horses go." They both kicked the manure and the manure went bouncing ahead of them.

The young man tired of living with these people who ate only human flesh and after a time he ran away.

—Archup

(Stella LaRose, translator)

The Cannibals

There were two groups of people who lived to the west. A man of one group said to another, "Let us hunt mountain sheep." They had bows and arrows. There was a main trail where they traveled back and forth on foot. They went as fast as a horse. The one who had suggested the hunting trip said, "I might just as well be an animal. They die in their tracks. They go so far in one direction and die. Another comes from another direction and dies."

The two men started digging and dug a place big enough to sit in. Around the edge of the hole they put a lot of sagebrush. They were right by the trail where they could shoot at anyone who went by. They had holes in the side of the sagebrush to shoot through. When it was complete the two men sat down in the hole. One man watched one way, the other watched the other. A man came along the trail. He had a bow and arrows on his back. He was going visiting. When he was near the blind, they shot and killed him. They took him to one side of the trail, butchered him, cooked and ate him. They roasted his head in the coals. They said it was very good meat.

They killed many people this way. Sometimes two travelers would come along together and they would shoot both of them. They took all the meat off the bones of their victims and then they would lay side by side the heads of all the people they killed.

The two groups of people had formerly used this trail to go back and forth on their visits to each other. Now they only went one way and never returned. The cannibals hung the quivers of their victims in a row near where they kept the bones.

There was an old man, his wife, son, and daughter who lived in one of the groups. The old woman said, "Don't you think our food is getting low? The people in the other bunch always fish this time of year. I think we should go visit them and have some good fish to eat." So they set out on the trip.

They went along the trail. There were too many of them for
the two cannibals to shoot them, so they came out of their
blind and were standing in the trail when the travelers came
along. The family stopped and looked beyond them to where
they saw a lot of dried meat hanging in the brush. The old
woman said, "Let us keep on going," but the old man said,
"No, I think that as long as there is meat in sight, we should
stay. I think we should stay with these two men tonight." He
persuaded his family to stay.

They camped not far from the two cannibals. The old
man built a fire. He told his daughter, "You better go visit the
two men. They will give you some of their dried meat." The
girl said, "I am afraid of them. They look dangerous to me."
Her parents insisted on her going, though she was unwilling.
She tried to get her father to go. The old man said, "I have to
fix a brush shelter for the night. I have no time to go. You go,
daughter."

The girl went to the camp of the two men. One of them
was fixing his bow. She sat down by them. She looked in the
brush and saw many quivers hanging in a row. Then she
looked at the ground beneath them and saw all the skulls. She
began to get frightened when she saw the human heads. The
man who was fixing his bow said, "Don't you think our eye fat
is about done now?" The other man got up, looked, and said,
"It is burned." He started knocking the burned part off. The
other said, "My meat has no fat on it. Perhaps some of your
dried meat might have fat." So the first man went to his row
and got some meat with fat, which he gave to the girl. She
thought, "This must be human flesh." She left. As she went
over a little knoll she heard one of the men say, "Look, what
fat meat she will make."

Her father had completed the shelter. "Here is the meat
you sent me for. It is human flesh." She threw the meat
down and said to her mother, "This is human flesh. When I
was over there I saw lots of skulls and lots of quivers hanging
in a row. They had human flesh drying. This meat they gave
me is human flesh. When I had gotten a little distance from

there I heard them smacking their lips and talking about what fat meat I would make. While I was there they had a human roast cooking. One of the men looked at it. It was round, like a human head."

The old woman began to cry. The old man said, "Don't cry too loudly. Are you sure you are telling the truth?" "Yes, I know they have been killing people and eating them." The old man said, "Keep quiet. We will wait until it gets dark and they will not see us running away. We will go back home. I will pretend to be getting wood for the night." He gathered wood.

Night came. They built a big fire. The man lit the fire and saw that the night was very dark. His family prepared to leave. The old woman said, "I have been watching those men. Every now and then they peek out and look up here." The old man said, "Get ready. Get on your hands and knees and crawl and we will get by their place. Then you run ahead and wait for me. I will start talking and hold their attention. Then I will run on and meet you."

They crawled until they got by the men's camp and they ran and waited at the appointed spot. The old man stayed and kept piling wood on the fire. Then he went away. He waited halfway and watched the fire. It burned down to coals. The cannibals were watching the fire, and when it burned down they thought the people had gone to sleep. They crept up there. One of them went on one side of the shade, the other came around the other side. They had their bows and arrows, ready to kill, but they discovered no one was there. They wondered how the people had discovered their plot and how they had escaped.

The old man ran to the place where he expected to find his family and then he asked aloud where they were. His wife answered, "Here we are." He told them how the two men had gone to their camp to kill them. "We got away just in time."

They went on until they came to the camps of the other group. They saw a fire and went to it. The old man called a greeting and was answered from within the tent. He asked, "Where is your chief's tent?" He was told it was where the fire was.

They went to the chief's tent, opened the door, and saw the chief. He greeted them and said, "Where did you come from?" The old man told where they had come from and described their journey. He told about the two cannibals on the trail and their dried meat. "My wife wanted to come on," he said, "but I said, 'Who wants to go on where here are two men with plenty of meat.' I made my wife stop there and sent my daughter visiting so that they might give her some meat. She did not want to go, but we persuaded her. She was gone some time and then came back with dried meat. When she came she threw the meat onto the ground and said, 'Do you want human flesh?' She told how, while she was sitting there, she saw lots of dried meat and quivers hanging up and skulls on the ground. They had one head in the coals, roasting. She told us how she overheard them talking about what fat meat she would make."

The chief said, "Yes, many of our men have gone in that direction and never returned. I have not had any news from that direction in some time. Maybe those cannibals have been killing our men. Perhaps that is as far as our men got." The chief went out of the tent and said, "I will call all the men together and tell them the news." He called, "A visitor has come and he has news." Many men came to the chief's tent and the old man told his story again to the other people. They said, "Yes, many of our men have gone visiting and never returned." They named the men who had disappeared. "Maybe that is what has happened. They have been eaten." They decided it was the son-in-law of a certain man who was one of the villains, and the son-in-law of another man who was the second.

They all believed the story the old man told. The old man said, "The quivers are there, but all that is left of the men is bones. Your people are all dead."

They thought that if a group of men had gone by the

blind, the cannibals would have persuaded them to stay over-night and killed them in their sleep. They planned to send two messengers by another trail to carry the news to the other group. The chief said, "These two men can go. I don't know what the cannibals will do when they run out of food." The chief told the two messengers to tell the people of the other group never to use the dangerous trail. He said, "The canni-bals will turn up somewhere when they run out of meat. Wherever they are found, they must be killed. We are going fishing. If they come here we will have to kill them. One of them has a sister here and they might come to her camp." The husband of this woman was at the meeting and they warned him not to tell his wife anything about the cannibals.

The two messengers went by a roundabout way to the camps of the other group. They said there, "Two men went out to hunt mountain sheep and never returned. They have been on the trail all this time. (What they meant by *mountain sheep* was *people*.) Our people never got any farther than the blind they built on the trail. There have been many of our people set out to visit there and they have never returned to us." They named some of the vanished people. They said that when the cannibals ran out of meat they would show up somewhere. Then the two messengers went home by the same way they had come.

At last the cannibals ran out of meat. They did not think about the family that had escaped them that night. They were not suspicious that they had been found out. They did not de-stroy the quivers or bones of their victims. They left them there and went to the camp of the sister of one of the men. Everyone was quiet, there was no excitement. One of the group called out, "Come on, we are going up here to finish our fishing." That was the way they had planned to get the cannibals.

When they got there the chief told them that the canni-bals were coming later on. "Scatter yourselves about. Pre-tend to be shooting with your bows. Some of you, sit down. The cannibals will probably sit down. One of them may ask, 'I believe this bow can shoot the farthest. It is a strong bow.' Then one of you can take the bow to examine it and pass it from one to another until it is some distance from its owner. One of the men who is pretending to fish can call, 'Let's get them!' The cannibals will think it means to get the fish, but it will mean to get the cannibals."

At last the two cannibals came. First they did not come near. Then they came a little nearer and gradually they came to the place where all the men were. They watched the men shooting with their bows and arrows. Finally they went and sat down with a group of men. One of the cannibals had a very long bow, the other's was shorter. One of the men sitting there said, "Let's see your bow. It is a handsome one. I believe it would shoot farther than any bow around here." The bow was made of mountain sheep horn. Then, some of the other men got the bow from the other cannibal in the same fashion. The second bow was of wood. One of the men who was shooting had said, "Let me try your bow." He tried it and said, "See how the arrow just flew from the bow." The man who was pretending the watch the fish cried, "Now let's get them."

The men on each side of the cannibals grabbed them and stabbed them with their knives. The owner of the wooden bow was killed first. He was stabbed in the heart. The other cannibal was a big man. He almost got away. He put up a good fight even after he had been stabbed. They got him down and crushed his head with an ax. They killed them both and left them lying there.

Then they went home. The man who was married to the sister of the cannibal told her how they killed her brother because he had been eating human flesh. She began to cry and cry and her husband said, "Where is your son? They killed him and ate him."

Next morning they all went to the cannibals' camp and two men were sent to the other group of to tell them to come and help identify the quivers. They found the quivers still hanging there and the skulls all piled up. They identified the quivers. The people from the other group came and they all cried over their dead. They saw where the cannibals had dug their pit and hid. They said, "This is where the cannibals hid and killed our people."

[Archup stated that he learned this tale from Kurump Longhair's husband, a Shoshone.]

—Archup

(Stella LaRose, translator)

The Supernatural Wife

The people were camped. They saw Bear coming. One said, "I will bet he is drunk." Bear was the first one to make whiskey and he always made trouble for the other animals. When Bear drew near, somebody said, "When Bear comes, tell him, 'Here is Bear. When he is drunk he is the best-natured person.'" Bear came and said, in response to the remark, "Yes, that is the way I am." Usually Bear was rough and stamped and scratched, but this time he was good. One of the people there, Deer, asked Bear if he had seen his son. Deer's son had vanished. "No," said Bear in a loud voice. There was a poor Mexican there, in ragged clothes. His toes were sticking out of his shoes. Bear asked the Mexican not to tell that he, Bear, had killed Deer's son down in the gulch. Deer asked everybody about his son but no one had seen him. They all hunted for some trace of him but could find none. Everyone searched. They offered Bear a reward if he could find any trace.

They began to think Bear had killed him. They wanted something to prove it. Bear refused every reward they offered. Deer offered to give the Mexican a wishing glass if he found his son. The Mexican went to the spot where the son lay and found him all fly-bloated. He kicked him in the foot and said, "Get up. Why are you lying here?" The young deer got up. The Mexican put him on his back and took him down to camp. Deer gave the Mexican the wishing glass. He took it and went away. He wondered what it was. He sat and talked to that glass and he wished for good shoes, a coat, hat, pants, shirt. Everything came to him. He put on his new clothes and threw away his ragged ones.

On his journey he came upon a big river. On the bank were two hawk sisters. One of them was mean. The Mexican had seen beforehand in his glass that he would meet the two girls and that he should take their clothes and jewelry. He took their clothes and the girls begged him to return them. One of the girls flew away. He returned the other's clothes. They went down the river together. Evening came and they slept together. The Mexican prayed to the glass for bedding and dishes and food. In the morning, when the girl awoke, she found herself on a bed with coverings on her. They had all the food they wanted. They ate, then they went on, leaving everything behind them.

The girl told the man never to call her "Whore," but to call her by her name, which meant "Shreddings-of-cedar-bark-woman." When night came, the Mexican prayed again to the glass and they got a completely furnished house. The girl went out of the door and saw corrals and chickens. Next morning the man milked the cow. The house was full of food. When the man came near the house, he called, "Whore-woman," and the girl was angry and did not answer him. The girl did not have her jewelry on. She said nothing. She put on her jewelry and flew away.

The Mexican followed her. He wanted to find her. He saw a fire in the distance and he went to it. The old woman there said, "Where are you going?" "I am hunting for my wife." "What are you going to eat? I have no food." He went on, and after a time, he camped for the night.

Next day he traveled all day looking for his wife. When he met an old woman, she would say, "Where are you going, my grandchild?" and he would say that he was hunting for his wife. He went on and on. He went to every fire he saw and asked for his wife. One old woman he met said, "Where are you going, my grandchild? My husband died. My son died and

I am here, all alone." He told her he was searching for his wife, Shreddings-of-cedar-bark-woman. The old woman told him that his wife was far away. She said, "Her home is on the other side of the mountain. There is a shining place there. That is where she lives."

The old woman then said, "There are four children play- ing not far from here." The Mexican said he would go and see them. The children were running races. He went to the chil- dren and said, "What game are you playing?" "Oh, we are just playing." One little boy said, "We play this game." He put his hat on his head and he vanished. Another boy said, "Here is another game." He got a stick and he said "Tausits!" and away he went, far, far away. Then he shouted "Tausits!" and was back again. He said, "We even revive the dead. When anyone dies we restore them."

They put down their magic things and had a race. The man took all their things. He called "Tausits!" and away he went. He drew near to the mountain. He saw another fire. An old woman was all alone. She was grinding something. She said, "I have nothing to eat. Where are you going?" The man said, "I am hunting for my wife." The old woman said, "They live far away. You will have to climb this mountain and then look far off. My husband died not long ago, also my son and my daughter." The man said, "Where are they? Lead me to the place where you put them." The old woman took him to the graves of her family and said, "This is my son. This is my daughter." The man hit each place twice with his stick and the dead arose. The Mexican stayed with them that night and next morning he went on his way.

He called "Tausits!" twice and arrived on top of the mountain. He looked down and saw the desert. In the middle of the desert he saw a shining place. He went down the hill, called "Tausits!" and flew off.

He stopped at another campfire where he met a group of people. An old woman said, "Where are you going?" "I am searching for my wife." The old woman said, "She lives a long way off." He replied, "This is what I do," and he put on his magic hat and disappeared. They looked for him but they could not find him although he was still there. The old woman said, "Hawk Mother is very disagreeable. I don't know how you will manage her. Your wife is all right, but her sister who wears a green dress is very mean. Your wife will be on the north side of the camp and her sister on the south side."

He went on his way and arrived at his wife's home in the late afternoon. The old woman was at the door. She was making grease bread. The man put on his hat, became invisible, and ate her bread. The old woman said, "What is happening to my grease bread? It is vanishing." The man went past her and went to his wife.

The girl came down to supper. She was getting extra bread to take to her husband. The old woman said, "What are you going to do with that extra bread? Did your husband come?"

Next morning the old woman said, "Your husband better go hunt buffalo today." Old Hawk Woman was very cross. The young girl said to her husband, "Take this magic thing. When you see the buffalo, just say that you want it to die and it will die." He did this and the buffalo also butchered itself by magic and packed itself home.

When he delivered the meat the old woman said, "Now I want your husband to fence the lot our brother was fencing." The girl said, "Take an ax. When you hit the tree, say, 'All the trees fall,' and they will all fall. Then say, 'All trees separate themselves for a fence.'" So the fence was built. When he returned, the old woman said, "Is he through building the fence?" "Yes." Then the old woman said, "How is that man managing to get the best of me? He is beating me. Is it with your help, daughter?"

Then the old woman wanted him to put barbed wire up. That also went up by magic. Then the old woman said, "Is he through fencing already?" "Yes." The old woman was angry and said, "Now I want him to level off the mountains." His wife told the man to go do it. He knocked the mountains down and made an extensive flat. The old woman was very angry.

She said, "I will try something else. Let him go way up on the cliff and get me a dipper of birds' tears." His wife told him, "Take my horse. He has a sore back, but he will carry you. When you get to the bottom of the cliff, kick him and make him run. He has been there before. When you get up on top of the cliff, say, 'I want a dipper of birds' tears.'" The young man did all this and brought back the dipper of birds' tears. The old woman was very angry. She wanted him to fail.

Because she was so angry, she wanted him to be arrested. They came and got him. An old, bony cat sneaked in the jail with him. The Mexican was tied in his cell. The mice were eating his clothes. Before he went to jail, his wife took his magic glass. He was unaware of this and had not minded going to jail, thinking he had his wishing glass with him. He asked for the lock of the jail to open, but nothing happened and he discovered he did not have the glass. He could do nothing.

He said to the mice, "My friends, don't chew my clothes." He said to the cat, "Go ahead and eat the mice." Then he heard the cat catching the mice. He spoke to the mice, "I wish my friends to help. Take the magic thing my wife put in my pocket and carry it to her house and exchange it for my own magic glass. It is on the wall. I will do anything I can for you." The mice said they were too big to do this. They were afraid they would get caught. He asked some bugs, but they could not do it. Then he asked Spider, who is always climbing the walls.

Spider went on the errand and the mice followed to watch him. The mice were chattering and squeaking. Spider went into the house and the girl paid no attention to him. He climbed up the wall and changed the magic things. He brought the Mexican his own magic possession and as soon as the man had it, he said, "I want the lock to open." It opened immediately. Then he wished for food with which to feed the animals who were in the jail with him and immediately there was plenty of food. The cat grew big and fat. The man and the cat left the jail.

Then the man wished for a store. He said, "You people, Mice and Spider, can live in the store and have everything free." Then he went to his wife's house. Next morning the old woman wanted him to make a bridge across a deep canyon. The cat went with him while he built the bridge.

Next the old woman wanted him to go to her brother's place. There was a boiling spring there and the young girl thought that the old woman wanted her husband put in the spring. The Mexican and his wife rode there on her horse. There was a big, hot lake. The old woman's brother wanted the Mexican to get in the lake, after he had gone in himself and lost his skin. The girl said to her husband, "Remove your clothes near my horse. Take some of the sore from the horse's back and rub it on your neck." He did this and was able to swim safely in the boiling lake. The other man died after he had come out.

The old woman shouted that she wanted his head chopped off. He went to the horse and, again, put some of the sore on his neck. The tool that was to cut his head off broke and he walked away uninjured. The old woman was angry and she chased him. The girl had her magic stuff with her and she and her husband fled. The old woman almost caught them but the girl threw back her looking glass, which turned into a big canyon between them and the old woman. The old woman managed to cross it. When she drew near, the Mexican put on his magic hat and he and his wife disappeared. Where did they go? They were right there.

The old woman was very angry. "They killed my brother. I will surely get them." Every time the old woman almost caught up to the young couple, the girl threw something back. A comb turned into a wilderness of brush that delayed the old woman. A needle was thrown while the girl said, "I wish it would turn into prickly-pear cactus." It did, but the old woman finally got through it. Then the girl threw a second looking glass that turned into a long ice lake. The girl and her husband watched the old woman's horse slipping and sliding on the ice. The old woman got dirt, which she put down for the horse to walk on. She led him and they got across. The girl said, "I am going to kill my mother." The old woman was yelling and shouting. She was very angry.

Next time they made a big lake appear in front of the old woman and the girl said, "Now I am going to kill her." She had made the lake by throwing a third looking glass. The old woman and her horse were swimming across the lake when the girl threw a little piece of glass that ripped the old woman to pieces. She floated to the bank and lay there. "I am going to let her lie there a long time," the girl said. Then she added, "I had nothing else to throw, that was the last. Perhaps if we revive the old woman, now she will behave differently." So they nudged her foot, and the wounds healed, and she woke up. "Oh, I have been asleep." From that time on she was different. She joined the Mexican and his wife and they traveled on together.

They found a good place for a farm, beside the river. The Mexican wished and there were houses, corrals, and fences.

—MARY WASH
(Stella LaRose, translator)

The Origin of Agriculture

There was a rooster out on the flats. There was a Mexican. The Mexican heard Rooster crowing and he went to him. He said, "Come with me, I want you to be mine." Rooster replied, "All right, I will be yours." The Mexican took him home with him. Rooster talked to him. He said, "I always crow early in the morning. Next time I crow it is just getting light. Then next time is just before sunrise. Then you can get up, it will be daylight. After sunrise I will crow again. Then you can prepare your meal and eat. I will crow again when the sun is part-way up. Then I will crow again just before noon. Then when I crow, prepare your meal and when I crow again, you can eat."

Every time the Mexican prepared a meal he would say, "Come and eat." Rooster would eat with him. "In the afternoon when the sun gets down a little I will crow and I will crow again when the sun goes down. After I crow for the last time, it will be dark and we must go to bed." That is how they lived. They used to eat together.

The Mexican said, "I am going visiting. You stay here." The Mexican went to visit his people. One of the men there said to him, "Will you fence this place for me? I want you to do this. If you do not do it, I will kill you." The man did not reply, he did not say whether he would or would not. He went home. He told Rooster, "There was a man there who wanted me to fence his place for him and I did not do it. What do you think about it? He told me he would kill me if I did not do it. Do you think that is all right?" Rooster said, "It does not sound good to me." The Mexican said, "Shall we run away from here and go to another place? I don't feel safe. I do not want to be killed." Rooster agreed, "All right, we will go some other place."

They started on their journey and came to a big river. The man said, "How will we get across?" "I don't know," said Rooster, "Can't you make a boat?" The man tied some sticks together, but it would not serve as a boat. He had nothing with which to cut the sticks even. He had no saw. While they were there someone came down the river and asked what they were doing. "I am trying to make a boat." The other man said, "I know someone who can make a boat easily. Why don't you go see him? He will make you a boat in a short time." "I will go see him in the morning."

Next morning the Mexican went to see the boatmaker. He told Rooster to wait for him. He went to the house and saw the man, who was Beaver. "What do you want?" said Beaver. "I came to get you to make me a boat." Beaver agreed to go with him. They went to the place where Rooster was waiting. The Mexican had been trying to hollow out a log. Beaver said, "This will not do. I will make you another." He got a bigger log and the Mexican said, "How are you going to hollow out this huge log?" Beaver said, "There is a man who lives on the other side of my place. He can help. Tomorrow morning I will go see him and I know he will help." Next morning Beaver went to this man's place and found him at home. "What is it?" "I want you to come back with me. I am trying to make a boat." "All right, I will go with you."

They went and looked at that big log and went to work. Beaver's friend pecked out a hollow in the log. He was a woodpecker. He made a big hollow and there was a canoe. He left a perch for Rooster to sit on. Woodpecker said, "Where are you going?" "We want to cross the river." Woodpecker went home, but before leaving he said, "Get two sticks and move them this way and you can get across."

The Mexican said to Rooster, "We have our boat. Shall we go?" and Rooster replied, "Yes, we better go." They got in the boat. Rooster sat on his perch and they pushed into the river. Rooster said, "Let's keep right on down the river. If we just cross over to the other side you might be killed. If we stay on the river we will leave those people far behind."

So they went down the river as far as they could, until they came to a rocky canyon. They went to the bank and got out of the boat. They stayed there. Rooster said, "This is a good place. The land is level, why don't you smooth it off." The Mexican worked every day and got the ground smooth. Rooster stayed in the brush and crowed at the times he had said he would crow. Rooster said, "Dig holes in the ground," and the man did so. He then told the man to sit down. Rooster put his head down and something came out of his mouth. He spit out something into each of the holes. He said, "The first that I spit out was corn, the other things are wheat, oats, watermelons, muskmelons, cabbage, peas. I planted all the different kinds of seeds." Everything that is planted now he planted then. He spit out more seeds and told the man to sow the oats first, then the wheat. Every time he spit there was a heap of seeds.

He told the man to cover all the seeds. Then he had him dig ditches along the sides of the field for irrigation. The man made the ditches. Then everything was all done. He had to irrigate next. The plants began to come up. They grew rapidly. In the fall everything was ripe. Rooster said, "Oats is good feed for horses. Wheat will be ripe soon and you can grind it into meal and cook and eat it. We will make a fire and parch the corn. You can then grind it and cook it like mush. Watermelons will be red in the center when they are ripe. Muskmelons will be yellow inside. You can cook the peas. They are good to eat."

Rooster told him to cook everything. "Some things you grind, some you boil. You cut the tops of the grain off and pound it with sticks. You husk the corn and dry it and put it away for winter. Now I have told you about everything. Be sure to save a little of each kind of seed for next year."

Rooster went back to the brush. He would crow every morning. One night the bird went to sleep and the man sat up alone. On the sides of their place were cliffs. Rooster had showed the man how to make tobacco out of corn husks. He used the fine husk next to the corn. He taught him how to make a corncob pipe. When the man was sitting alone, he noticed what seemed like a light in the cliff. It seemed to him that someone occasionally walked in front of the light. He wondered who it was. He took a stick and pointed it to where he saw the light.

Next night when he and Rooster were eating, the stick still lay there, pointing to the light, but the man did not tell Rooster anything about the light. After the bird went to bed, the man went toward the light. He crossed the river and climbed to where the fire was. He could hear someone coming to meet him. He stood there looking up and saw a woman. "What kind of woman are you?" "I am a Mexican woman, what are you?" "I am a Mexican, also. Where are you going now?" "I am going to get water from the spring."

The man said, "I will go with you. Where do you live?" "I live up on the hill." They got the water and went up steep, rock steps to climb the hill.

There were many people there. Her husband and children and sisters were there. They asked him where he lived. "Across the river." They said, "We do not travel around in the daytime, we hide." They were afraid of somebody who kills. The man said, "I watched this light, I thought there was someone here." He took out his tobacco and started smoking. They said, "How good that smells. We like the smell of your tobacco. Let us try some of it." So the man rolled a cigarette for his host. They asked him where he got his tobacco. He told them about his farm. "I have everything in my garden." This surprised them. They had not known that there was anyone else near them. "My corn is ready to eat," he said.

The man said to the girl who had gone after water, "You better marry this man." The Mexican stayed with the girl that night. He did not go home. He got up early in the morning and went home to the place where Rooster was. He got breakfast ready for Rooster. He called him to eat and Rooster came, but he stayed outside. He did not come in. He acted very strange when he finally came in. I guess the man smelled differently. Rooster did not stay to eat. He went back to the brush and he crowed when it was time for him to crow. Night came and Rooster did not come to the house.

The man went to his wife's place. Early next morning he came home, got breakfast, and called Rooster, but Rooster did not crow that morning. He looked for him but he could not find him. He tracked him and followed him until he got into timbered country. At noon he could hear Rooster crowing far off, but he could not find him. He came home and spent the night with the girl. He took corn and showed her how to cook it, to parch it. They all liked the flavor of the corn.

Early in the morning he went home and hunted again for Rooster. He could not hear him, nor could he find him. He found a nest with a lot of eggs in it. He took the eggs home

with him and put them away. One day he found they had
hatched and chickens come out of them. That is where the
chickens came from. Rooster left the eggs for him. When he
had lots of chickens he brought his wife home.

This is where everything came from.

—ARCHUP

(Stella LaRose, translator)

The Ragged Man

A long time ago there was a man who was ragged. He was a
queer man. He had scars burned on his stomach. He was all
scratched and torn on his face and body. He burned himself,
making white scars.

A woman told her brother to get that man, she wanted to
marry him. The ragged man did not know how to ride a
horse, he fell off. The brother tied him on a horse when he
first fell off, but he fell off again. Then the brother tied him on
again more carefully. The horse trotted and the man learned
how to ride horseback. Then he got on a horse all alone.

He was a good man. He killed many buffalo. He told the
brother, "When I kill a buffalo, you butcher him." He was a
good man, even if he was ugly.

—PEARL PERIKA

(Mamie Alhandra, translator)

Badger and Fly

There was once a little Mexican boy about three years old.
His father and mother were dead and Siants took care of him
and raised him to manhood. She used to feed him. Badger
asked Siants if he could have her for a wife. She said, "You
are not accustomed to my kind of food. Today is a difficult
day. We are going to have a peyote meeting at my place tonight." Badger said he did not eat peyote and he went away.

He went on and came to a place where there were a lot of tipis. He saw a young girl who wore a white apron over her private parts. He thought, "There is a young girl, perhaps I can marry her." Her name was Fly. He had made a necktie on his way. She thought it pretty. He grabbed her with his long nails. They were married. Wasp came to their tipi and said, "Oh, you are married." "Yes, I married this man." Wasp said, "Where did he come from?" "Oh, he came along and I was tired of chopping wood, so I married him and now he can chop wood for me."

Badger said, "I am going to clear this land for her." He worked every day, grubbing that brush. He made a wooden plow and he would plow. His wife came along behind, whipping him as one does a horse. Badger got so tired he went to sleep and slept for two days.

One day while he was asleep his wife went to the brook and made mud horses with wooden sticks for legs. She talked to them and told them she wanted them to be real horses. She told them to be over a certain hill the next morning. That night she made a little corral. Next morning she awakened her husband and told him to look over on the hills. "Can't you see anything?" "No, I can't see anything." Then she told him to wash his face and open his eyes. When he did this he saw the horses. She told him to get the horses and put them in the corral. She was tired from the effort of making the horses, so she stayed at home while her husband plowed.

One day when she was sleeping, Mosquito came along and said, "What are you doing, sleeping?" She said, "I got tired of helping my husband plow, so I made him some horses and now I can sleep." Mosquito said, "Maybe I can help your husband."

They farmed together. This woman had magic power. She would sew weeds together and they would turn into blankets. She made a bed for the hired man. They had no meat, so she took the potato worm, told him she was hungry, and Worm got food that turned into meat. She ground up seeds and they turned into flour. She wanted a child. She was

lonesome and called the worm "Grandmother." Grandmother made a little mud baby. When they went to bed, she
thought, "Early in the morning I will get that baby and it will
be a real baby then." The old woman got up early and got the
baby, which she laid at the door of the tent. Then the old
woman crawled in under the side of the tent and lay down and
slept. The baby began to cry and the young woman got up
and got that baby.

Mosquito wanted to see the baby. He said, "You better
nurse that baby," and she did. The baby was so hungry that
every time she tried to take her breast away it would cry. So
her husband had to get breakfast while she nursed the child.
She loved that baby.

There was a doctor's house over on the hill where Badger lived. They made a wagon and took the baby there.
There was a pregnant woman there.

While the men were out in the field they saw smoke in
their tipi and they thought perhaps Fly had come back from
the doctor's. At noon they came to the tent. Mosquito looked
in and saw that there were things cooking. He saw a great,
big woman who seemed to be in pain.

Mosquito ran to Badger, who was taking care of the
horses, and told him about the strange woman. They went to
the tipi and asked her if she were pregnant and she said,
"Yes." Mosquito got on his horse and took that woman
horseback to the doctor's. When they got there everyone
was surprised and said, "Oh, Mosquito, did you get married?" He said, "No," and explained. The woman gave birth
to twins. [The narrator of this tale has twin daughters.] One
of the babies had a lot of hair and the other had no hair at all.

Wasp was the nurse. Mrs. Badger (Fly) was well now
and ready to leave the hospital and she said, "Tell my husband to come after me."

While Mosquito was on the way home, someone called
to him from under the cliff. It was Turtle. Mosquito went to
see him and found that Turtle had a fine house under the cliff,
with a glass front. It was a store. Turtle said, "What do you

want? I have everything in my store." Mosquito loaded down his horse with flour and all kinds of food. It was all free. When he got home, he told Badger to go get his wife. The hospital was filling up fast.

Badger got his wagon and went for his wife. On the way home someone called to them. It was Turtle. They went to see him and he gave them all kinds of things with which they loaded the wagon. When they got home Fly went to the garden and saw that everything was growing well. She ran to her husband. She was so proud of him that she made love to him. So they made love to each other and lay down there and went to sleep.

The baby never cried. It slept all the time. While they were asleep the old woman thought she would fool them. She put the baby under the bed. They awoke, missed their baby, and began to cry. Fly fainted. The old woman laughed and said, "What is the matter?" Fly said, "Oh, I have lost my baby!" "Why, what is this under the bed?" Fly ran and found her baby and was very happy.

The two men went to irrigate. Pretty soon Badger said, "I must go back to my wife." He went and they loved each other until they were very tired and then they went to sleep.

When Mosquito saw his friend go to sleep with his wife, he returned to work. He killed a deer and packed it home and they had plenty of meat. When he got home he found that the woman who had born twins had been there. She asked the old woman if she could have Mosquito for her husband. Grandmother said she would speak to Mosquito about it and asked who was the father of the babies. The woman said, "They are Mosquito's babies. He used to come to my house before he came here." Mosquito said, "All right, if that is the way she feels about it, I will take her for a wife." He married her.

Night came and they went to bed. Before they were up in the morning, Meadowlark came. He and Magpie had just been married. Meadowlark said, "Oh, my sister, I have been looking all over for you." Breakfast was ready and they all sat down and ate. Meadowlark choked and said, "This is the first time I have eaten for a long time. My throat is tight and I cannot swallow very well." His wife kept putting her finger down his throat to open it up. The second meal they had, he felt better. He ate plenty then and then grew sleepy. Fox was their dog.

Meadowlark and his wife went to look at the garden, and they were so pleased with it that they wanted to stay there and live with Badger so that Meadowlark could see what he could raise. They decided to live with Fly, and Fly made a house and bedding for them. Meadowlark's wife began to have pains. She was pregnant. They told her where Dr. Badger's hospital was, so she went there and gave birth to a white-bellied boy.

Every day another family came and wanted to live there. Soon there was a village there. Bald-headed Hawk wanted them to move camp, but they did not want to go. They did not trust Hawk. Badger said, "I will fix a trap for him." He made a rope out of soapweed and put a loop in it. Next morning he heard something squealing and found Hawk caught in the noose.

They let him stay in the trap for a long time. They waited until he stopped crying and then went to him and found him dead. He had chewed out his tongue. Hawk was a bad man with women. He grabbed them around the neck and choked them. He murdered girls. They caught him, cut his hair off, and rubbed soapweed and sand into his scalp until it was sore. No hair grew on his head after that. That is how he got his bald head.

Old Badger Woman said, "That Hawk was here, bothering me." They told her he would not do that anymore and described how they killed him.

A long-legged water bird, who had a dark blue suit and a purple hat, lived alone. She used to make big loaves of bread. Hawk came to visit this bird, he wanted to marry her. Heron did not want to marry him. She said, "At times I don't feel well, sometimes I faint. I am not healthy." She said that so that Hawk would leave her alone. She said, "It is almost time for me to go to the hospital." She wanted him to get rid of the idea of marrying her. She went to the hospital, but Hawk stayed at her place. He took the bread she had baked to his mother. Badger came to visit and he asked where Heron was. Hawk said she had gone to the hospital. "When will she be back?" "I don't know." Badger said, "It is strange that she would leave the place in your care and leave her bread. It seems queer to me."

When Heron came back from the hospital old Badger Woman came to see her. She had just seen a man with a pretty green shirt and she was very excited. He wore glasses. Heron decided she would like to marry this man. She asked him if he would farm for her and he agreed. Everything he planted grew fast. This man, Duck, was a good farmer. Everything ripened quickly. He decided to make a fence. Mosquito told him there were many thieves and advised him to make a trap. "No," said Duck, "I am going to fence my garden."

He took leaves and strung them together and melted some pine pitch and put it around his garden. In the night he heard someone shouting. Lion and Coyote were stuck in the pitch. Heron said, "I hear someone crying, let's go help them." Duck said, "No, I am going to punish them. Let them stay there for twenty days." They were caught with both their hands stuck in the pitch. They also caught old Badger in the pitch on the other side of the garden.

Duck said, "What are you doing? If you wanted something to eat, why didn't you come to my house? There is a lot of food there." He said to Badger, "Do you want me to turn you loose?" Badger said, "If you turn me loose and give me a melon, I will never steal again." Duck said, "I won't give you any of the melons in the field for they are green, but I will free you and you can come up to the house and get some ripe melons." He did the same for Coyote and Lion. Badger ate so much he vomited and almost died. When Badger felt better he wanted to stay there. When Coyote finished eating, he went a little way, turned and bowed to them, and then went away.

Badger stayed at this place where they had such good melons and helped with the work. He said, "I have roamed all over the country and I am tired. I have been to many places. In some places I was well treated, in some places badly. I am tired now and I think I will stay here."

After a while they heard news about Coyote and Lion. They were far away. They were starving. Their moccasins were all worn out and their feet were full of thorns. Their old grandmother thought them dead and put them between the rocks to burn them. She cried and mourned their death.

After she went away, Coyote and Lion got up and disguised themselves. They put pitch around their eyes and ashes on their heads so they would look old and gray. Coyote tied up his tail. They pretended to be a couple of old men. They came to the place where the old woman was and found her still weeping. They told her that they had come from a long way off and were tired and weary. They did not fool Mosquito, who studied them and finally said, "Aren't you two the grandchildren that the old woman is mourning?" They said, "Oh, no! Those two were young men. They never lived to grow old. They did not look like us." Mosquito kept on studying them. They were given watermelon to eat, and when it was finished, they asked for more. While they were eating, Coyote wished Mosquito would go to sleep. He wished so well that Mosquito fell asleep.

Coyote had one of the water-skaters for his dog. When Mosquito fell asleep, Coyote took his dog to the melon patch and threw him over the fence. The dog picked the melons and brought them to Coyote. He made several trips and they had a big pile of melons. They made Jackrabbit act as a mule and haul them. They had stolen quite a few before Mosquito and the others in camp woke up and discovered that a whole row of melons was gone.

They were very angry at Coyote and Lion. Butterfly came to Coyote and said, "Have you stolen those melons?

They look like Mosquito's melons." "Oh, no," said Coyote, "Mosquito did not plant anything. He steals from us. I do the farming. Also, that man lives with my wife. We are going home now. We were out hunting elk, that is why we brought this food with us."

Butterfly left and went to Mosquito's camp. "I have come to visit my brothers," he said. "What did you see on your way?" "I met a couple of men going elk hunting. Coyote told me you were living with his wife." "Oh," said Mosquito's wife, "I would not live with one of those two, they eat dead horses." Butterfly said, "They had a load of melons they brought from their garden. They had a little dog." "I wonder if Coyote did not toss his dog over the fence. I saw that dog's tracks in my garden." They made the fence higher then and put more gum on it so that the thief would get stuck the next time.

That evening Butterfly got sick. They made a shelter for him. They were going to hold a peyote meeting for him. They drummed and sang their best songs and Butterfly soon felt better. During the meeting a woman jumped up and said, "That dog is caught on the fence by his front leg. Coyote tossed him over the fence to get more melons." While the meeting was going on, Coyote had thrown the dog over the fence and it was caught. Coyote and Lion heard the singing and wanted to go to the meeting. Mosquito said, "I can feel that those two are coming here. One of you go to the door and ask them in."

So Coyote and Lion came in. They were disguised differently. The woman said, "What have you two been doing? This meeting has been going well. You tell the truth." Coyote said, "We have done nothing." The people kept on questioning and Coyote and Lion were ashamed and backed out of the meeting. The people followed them out. Now they knew who had stolen the melons. They could hear the crying of the dog caught in the fence.

Coyote and Lion disappeared. The people smelled a peculiar odor. Mosquito went to see what it was. He saw tracks and saw that Lion had beat Coyote to death. Coyote decayed immediately. Lion said, "You lead me into trouble." That is why he killed him. Mosquito had to drag Coyote off and he cut him in little pieces, which he threw in the creek, so he would not revive.

—LIZA MAYOR
(Stella LaRose, translator)

[Liza Mayor was at Archup's camp one day when Archup was telling stories and invited Stella and me to her camp, saying she could tell us lots of stories. She appeared to improvise a good deal as she went along, stopping for long silences or to tend one of the children. Stella would then remind her what she had just told.—Anne M. Smith]

A Complicated Tale

Coyote was a woman. She had a shade made of brush. She lived there alone. One day Bear came and wanted to marry her. She said, "All right, if you will hunt for me. I have nothing to eat." He went hunting and brought her food. She was eating but the food caught in her throat. She could not swallow. Bear told her to run around. She did and was all right. Bear told her to go dig up a certain plant that is food for bears. She gathered a lot of the plant for her husband.

Night came. Bear wanted to go to bed. While they were asleep a young deer came to their camp. "What are you doing, lying there in bed?" Then Dog came and found Bear. He came in and chewed up Bear. Coyote Woman was frightened and ran away. She cried, because Dog had killed her husband. She went into some bushes to hide and sat down astride White Bear.

White Bear said, "Are you the woman who was married to my brother?" She said she was. He said, "I shall take you for my wife. You must go with me. I live among the rocks." The woman sat there and began to scream. Bear said, "What is the matter?" She said, "I am afraid that Crow is going to kill me, that is why I am frightened." He grabbed Crow, hit him with a stick, and killed him. He tore him in pieces. The woman did not want to stay there for she was frightened. Bear was angry because she did not want to stay. He hit her and she ran away.

He could not track her because she was careful to walk only on rocks and sticks and did not leave any footprints. She came to a brook where there were a lot of cattails. "I wonder if he will find me if I sit in the water." She sat in the water and put up a red flag and Owl came and saw it. He wanted to know if she would not go to his home and be his wife. He said, "I live up on the hill among the rocks. It is hard to get up there."

While they were going to Owl's house she got sick and foam came out of her mouth. Perhaps her husband, Bear, had medicine that caused it. She died. Owl began to weep. He took her among the rocks to bury her. He began to put rocks on her.

While he was working, White Bear came. He had disguised himself by putting pitch on his eyes. White Bear said, "What are you weeping for?" "This is where my mother used to come and cry and I am alone now. That is why I am crying." White Bear said, "Did you see my wife around here?" Owl said, "No, I have not seen her, my friend." Little Turtle came up and said, "I saw your wife. She was running away over there, on that mountain." He was only jesting. Bear said, "Yes, that must have been my wife. I have been looking for her." White Bear went off in that direction to find his wife. He ran and ran until he could go no farther, then he fell down and died.

Owl and Turtle went after Bear and when they reached him, he was dead, with foam coming from his mouth. They got sticks and propped him up so that he looked as though he were standing. They thought perhaps a friend of his might come along and see him. Grizzly Bear came and smelled him all over, then hit him and said, "What are you standing here for? You used to beat me." He kept on hitting him. Grizzly Bear then told Owl and Turtle that he had killed his enemy and said, "That man is out of the way now. Come with me."

They went away together. They came to a brook. "Let's go swimming," said Bear. Owl and Turtle were frightened. They thought Bear wanted to kill them. They decided to fool him. They caused a lot of water to come down the stream. Bear was out in the middle of the creek and he was washed down under the water. Owl and Turtle ran away. Bear probably drowned.

They walked along and came to a place where berries grew. They found some weeds that are used for making soap and they ate them. Foam started to come from their mouths. They died. While they lay there, Rabbit came and found them. He wanted to help them, so he dragged them to a creek and got some water and washed out their mouths. The foaming stopped. When he got the soap out of Owl's mouth, Owl opened his eyes and said, "Oh, my friend. You saved my life. What can I give you for pay? Shall I give you my skin?" "No," said Rabbit, "I don't want any pay. I did not want to see you die." Turtle was jumping around. He had not quite recovered. Rabbit worked on him and he recovered. Turtle wanted to know how he could pay Rabbit, but Rabbit said he did not want any pay. He said, "Come now, you are all right now. Let's go."

They went on their way and met Brown Bear. She had a litter of young ones. She was in a *wickiup* full of bark, like an Indian woman. They said, "We have come a long way. We would like something to eat." The woman got alkali, which she used for flour. She made a big pile of bread and then she made gravy. When Rabbit took a mouthful he burned his mouth. The other two helped him. They said, "You did not feed us very well." Bear said, "That is what I have to live on. You have eaten my food and now you are complaining." She chased them away and clawed Rabbit's back, taking the skin off. His friends tied his fur back in place and went on.

They were looking for water. They went on until they

came to a brook. They were very tired and they died. First Turtle, then Rabbit, and then Owl died. While they were lying there Butterfly came along and wondered what was the matter. He looked at their feet and saw they were full of thorns. They had been so tired when they came to the brook they had not looked at their feet.

Butterfly pulled out the thorns and they all woke up. "My feet feel a lot better. I have been asleep." They began to run around and try their feet. They stayed at the place where they had been revived. Owl got sleepy and went to sleep. Turtle and Rabbit stayed awake. Grasshopper came along riding a pinto horse. He offered them his horse. They told him how they had come there with sore feet and Grasshopper suggested that they all get on his horse and continue their journey.

They got on the horse and continued their journey. They came to a camp where there was a woman grinding. The old woman got up. They heard sheep making a lot of noise. The boy who was herding them was her grandson. The old woman told him that strangers were coming and told him to hide the sheep. The boy drove the sheep down a hole in the ground. Owl and the others could not see where the sheep went. Owl said that there must be another entrance to the hole somewhere near. They kept on searching. The boy and the sheep went out the other entrance to the hole.

While they were hunting the sheep, the old woman hid all her possessions. She was afraid of these strangers. When Owl and his friends went to the place where the old woman's tipi had been, it had disappeared. "I wonder where it has gone. There was a tipi here when we passed this morning. I wonder where it has gone." Owl was a medicine man. He was on the ground and the ground told him, "When they have visitors, they always disappear like that."

They went on. They started down a slope. They were hungry because they had gotten nothing to eat at that camp that disappeared. They came to another camp and met a woman. "Grandmother," they said, "give us something to eat." "I am not your grandmother." They told her that the camp they had visited had disappeared and they had gotten nothing to eat. The old woman said, "That outfit is no good. You should not eat with them. They are selfish. What would you like to eat?" They said, "Anything at all."

The old woman set the table for them and brought meat and bread. "Why don't they start eating?" When they began to eat, the old woman went into the tipi and brought out more to eat, cakes and pies. They did not know what they were. "We don't eat that," they said. The old woman said, "They are good to eat, you should try them." They did. There was a little boy with the old woman and she told him to take a sack and go. He went, came back a different way, and brought a sack of melons with him. They were very pleased at having so much to eat. They were filled, for once.

They set off again. They felt miserable because they had eaten so much. Owl got sick, began to vomit, and finally died. The others cried and mourned. They bounced so hard on the horse that Owl's stomach burst. That is what killed him. The others wondered what the old lady fed them that caused Owl's illness, but the real reason was that he had eaten too much.

Coyote was with them. He also had eaten too much and he was the next to die. Grasshopper was all right and so was Butterfly. They had eaten just enough. They laughed at the others who were sick. "I wonder how far we are going," they said. They were far away from everybody. Butterfly said, "We will cry and cry for our father and then we will have to turn around and go back. We will try to find a shortcut." Grasshopper was so lonesome he fainted every once in a while. So they started home.

They camped out at night. They were crying one night when Mountain Lion came. "What are you crying for, my grandchildren?" He said he would join them and travel with them. When they went with Mountain Lion, the distance did not seem so far. They were home before they knew it. Lion asked the father of Grasshopper and Butterfly, "Where did you send these children? Why did you send them so far away from home?" The father said, "We have searched all over for them and we could not find them. It has been months and months since they went away. We have looked all over for them. We don't know where they have been." Lion said, "Don't ever send your children away. You have affection for your children. They might get sick and die far away. Don't ever send them away again." Then Lion went home.

It did not take Lion long to get home. He only camped two nights on the way. When he got home he went whistling to his wife. "Where have you been?" she said. "You have been away two nights." "Oh, I just took those two little boys who were crying to their home." She said, "I am glad you took them home. I hope next time their mother takes better care of them."

"Our food is running low," she said, "we have nothing to eat." Lion went hunting and he found some berry bushes loaded with chokecherries. He got the berries and one elk and one deer and took them home. His wife was happy, for she had plenty to eat again. She tanned the hides of the deer and the elk.

—LIZA MAYOR
(Stella LaRose, translator)

Lion

Elk Butterfly said to her grandmother, "Let's move camp. We are too far from people." She had a little brother about five years old. Their mother lived about twenty-five miles away. The children lived with their grandmother. The girl was unmarried. The brother was very smart. Lion came by and they found that Lion was the son of their grandmother's sister. When Lion found they were planning to move, he said, "Why don't you come and live with us?" The old woman said, "Yes, we are all relatives. We will come." When they moved to Lion's camp, his wife made them an elk-hide tipi.

Lion saw that they had nothing to eat so he got ready to hunt for his aunt. Another animal came there and he wanted to marry the young girl. Lion said, "Well, I need help around here. I agree if it is all right with the girl's grandmother." The old woman said, "Yes." Lion said, "He can go hunting with me." He asked if he had a gun. The animal said, "No. My horse got frightened and knocked his gun down and he did not have a gun." Lion gave him a gun and a spear and they went hunting together.

They brought home the meat and they all had plenty of meat. The old woman was happy. The men went hunting together every day and they brought home meat and berries. The women would dry and grind the berries. One day an old man and an old woman came. They had wandered around all their lives. Lion said, "They better stay here. You two have been traveling around all your lives. You are getting old now. You better settle here and stay." So they stayed and Lion did all the hunting for them.

Lion asked the old woman what her name was. She said it was Sand and the old man said his name was Chokecherries. Lion wanted his wife to give them their old tipi, so she set it up about fifty yards away for the old couple. They lived there. When Lion hunted the next day, he brought the old couple lots of meat and berries.

The old couple found that every morning there was less meat in their cache and thought someone stole it every night. When their food was reduced to very little they told Lion and he said, "Let it go, you may find out who it is." One day the old woman was out getting wood and the old woman was alone when the thief peeked into the tent. It was an old man with gray hair. The old woman ran and told Lion. "You better come and track this thief." The trail was very plain. Lion tracked him and finally caught up with him. Lion said, "You must not steal. You must not take other people's food. If you are hungry, come to me." He was so angry at the thief that he beat and killed him.

Lion and his group moved camp. They had a wagon, an

old Mexican wagon, a buckboard. They packed their goods in that wagon when they moved camp. The little boy took the horses along behind them. They met an old woman who was starving. She was so weak that she kept falling down. Lion said, "Wouldn't you like to have that old woman for your mother? She could help you around the camp." His wife said, "My mother isn't old and feeble like that." Lion said, "Well, we can call her 'Mother' and she can help you tan hides and look after the children." His wife said she thought that would be all right. So they caught up with the old woman. She was weeping. Lion got down and helped her up on the wagon. She said, "If you people want to take me, you will save my life. I am starving." They gave her lots of water and she vomited. Then they gave her food, which she vomited. Then she began to get over that starving feeling. She was shaking all over; she almost died.

They went on their way and finally came to a good place to camp. The old woman was a lot better than when they had found her. They ate their supper. A young woman came into the tent. She was wearing a white blanket. Lion's wife said, "What is the matter with you? Are you pregnant? You are wearing that blanket and it seems very big." She said, "No, I have just got a large stomach and it keeps on growing."

She lay down on the old woman's bedding and rolled around as if she were in pain but she said nothing. Finally she rolled over and lay on her back and all at once they heard a baby crying. She had borne a baby. The old woman was shouting, "She had her baby on my blankets." The old woman who had almost died of starvation wanted to take this woman for her daughter and Lion said, "All right. Maybe some day a man will come along and want to marry her and you will have a son-in-law." The old woman took the woman to her tent. They fixed a tent for the mother and dug a hole and fixed hot rocks in it for her to lie on. Lion got her a stick to use for scratching her head. They stayed in that place all winter until spring came.

Fox came to their camp and said, "I have a store down

here and you people better come down and buy things from my store." The old man went scouting around and brought back a big sow with her little ones. He had found some wild pigs. The women said, "Where did you find that animal with all the little ones?" "I found them straying around and I brought them home." The old woman said, "You better fix some kind of corral to keep them in." The old man said, "I made one the other day, in case I captured some animal." He took the pigs to the corral and shut them up.

Then he went wandering in the woods, humming to himself. A bird fell in front of him. The bird had come to tell the old man that someone wanted to see him. Fox had sent him to ask the old man to come to his store. He went there and Fox gave him everything he wanted. He had many things to carry home. They were all glad to see the old man return with the things. "Where did you get those things?" He told them they came from Fox's store. The old woman said, "I think I will take my buckskin down there and sell it." She went there, but Fox said, "No, I don't want to buy things from you. I want to give you things. I want to help you." He never charged them anything. He gave them everything they wanted.

The young woman with the baby disappeared. She ran away. She told people about Lion and every day many people came to Lion's camp to eat. There was plenty of food that Fox had given them from the store. The girl's mother came and they were all very glad. She said to Fox, "My friend, have you a store?" He said, "Yes, I have a store because I want to help feed all you people."

Lion said, "I am expecting more people. They have come a long way. When they come there will be wagon after wagon with white sheets over the top of them." They looked and they saw a long wagon train coming.

Coyote was there. He said he would build another store to help feed his people. Coyote built a store, but he was not generous with his goods. He never gave anything away. He charged for everything and he traded with the people. Elk

Butterfly was the real boss of the merchants. They sent Coyote away. They did not like his store.

They had only one mule to do the plowing. One man whittled out a stick for a plough and they plowed with that. Elk Butterfly told them they should farm, should plant seeds and get food that way. They planted everything for which they could get seeds and they irrigated their gardens from a spring. Everything grew well. They had fine melons and corn.

Fox went to visit one man and saw his fine garden. He wandered around and he saw some tracks, which looked as if many children had been there. Rabbit and Fox followed the tracks and caught the thieves with the things they had taken from the garden. Fox shouted and told them to drop everything. They dropped their spoils and ran to the creek. The thieves were Water Babies. They ran fast but Rabbit caught one little one, the darkest one of the lot. They kept him and after a while he got to be like them and was one of the tribe.

Lion's tent was handsomely painted in the back, outside. Lion said, "We should go see the garden, there might be more thieves there." The dark one said, "We don't steal in the daytime, we only come out at night." Lion said, "We will station two people there to stand guard." They made a rope out of soapweed and made noose traps around the garden.

During the night they heard some shouting. It was the Water Babies who had gotten caught in the rope. Many of them were caught, including one big dark one, like a Negro. He was the biggest one. Lion spent next day making a jail out of cattails. They put the Water Babies in the jail.

Lion would take them out, one at a time, for a walk. After a while they got used to him and got tame. They seemed to like him. The big black one, who was the leader, said, "One of my sons wants to marry your grandmother's daughter." Lion said, "He will have to wait a couple of years or more before he can think of marrying into our tribe." After Lion had gone he said, "Lion is too clever. I was planning on taking her under the water with us," but Lion was outside, listening. The Water Babies said, "Why don't we try to escape and go back to our home? We want to go home." After that, Lion would not take them out for a walk. He brought their meals to them.

They said, "What will we do? We have been out of the water for so long. We are used to being on earth." The big one said, "I am used to it too. I never like the water much, anyhow." When they decided they wanted to live on the earth and not go back to the water, Lion set them free. But some of them could not keep out of the garden. There were still noose traps there and they would get caught. Lion told the boys to stay around the camps and chop wood for the old women.

Lion went to the garden and found that they had caught a very big woman. The little ones had come from that woman. The Water Babies were so tame after Lion freed them that they did not think about their water home any more. They were a separate tribe and settled in one place. They had their children and raised their families. They farmed and their gardens were just as good as the others.

The Water Babies grew old. The big, dark one had curly hair that began to turn gray. He looked shabby and old. The Water Babies had had very pretty blue and green dresses when they lived in the water. After they came out on land they had no more pretty clothes. When they became humans they wore only g-strings. One of the Water Babies escaped and went back to the water. Another went after him and brought him back in jail. He sat in jail and cried and begged to be freed. They let him out and he did not try to go back to the water anymore. They told him if he ever ran away again he would have to stay in jail all the time. He said he would never run away again if they would let him marry a certain girl. They let him have her for his wife. After he married, he plowed and worked all the time.

The store man came and said, "Do you need anything to eat?" They decided to go down to his store and make him feed them. They went to Fox's store and he gave them all kinds of provisions. He told them to come back in six days and said he would then give them more food.

After a while an old man said, "Has six days passed yet?" They told him the six days were not yet up. Wolf got sick and the old woman said to her husband, "Why don't you doctor your grandson? Then he will get well quickly." So the old man doctored him and cured him. Finally the six days were up and they all went to the store again. They must have waited a day too long, for when they got there Fox and the store had gone. They were very disappointed. They hunted around to see if they could not find Fox, but he was gone. Finally they found Fox and they beat him until they killed him.

Someone else built a store. He was a good man also. He fed them. He did not have the store very long. He quit the business. He did not keep the store as long as Fox had.

—LIZA MAYOR
(Stella LaRose, translator)

The Woman and the Dog

Once there was a man with no children and he went hunting. His wife would make the dog have sexual intercourse with her. Every time he came home she would smell like dog urine. He found out that she was pregnant and so he made her a house someplace, and when it was time they turned out to be dogs; they came out one by one. All the people left her, and just one of them was human, the man's son.

—TECUMSEH MURRAY
(Josephine LaRose, translator)

Coyote's Wife

Once Coyote had a wife and after living with her for some time he noticed that she got tired of him being around. So,

one day he told her that he was going hunting. He left and
went to the nearest hill and sat down to watch her. Finally
she came and started to jump up and down. She did this for
some time, then left.

Day after day he used to say he was going hunting, but
he used to watch her instead. After a while he got tired of it
and went to see what it was all about and was curious to
know what made her jump up and down. It was a naup. He
got thorns and put them on the naup and left. The next day
he left again and she did the same thing, but after she sat
down this time, she did not get up. When she did get up she
could hardly walk home. After she reached home, she died.

—TECUMSEH MURRAY
(Josephine LaRose, translator)

Lizard Hand

Once there lived Lizard and Coyote. They got into a quarrel.
They were arguing about the ways of the people. They were
deciding on how many fingers they should have. Coyote said
they should only have four fingers, Lizard thought they
should have five, they would get along with five. And they
should have five toes too. They debated a long time about
this and finally Coyote gave in and they had five. So Lizard
won.

—ATWINE
(Stella LaRose, translator)

Mythical Times

A long time ago the birds were people. Siants was among
them then. They used to have many kinds of dances. Every
variety of bird had a song. Siants was very mean and used to
steal the children. Coyote was very mean also. That is the
way God made them. One of the birds flies when the wind

blows. He floats around up in the air. In the spring, when the wind is going to blow, the sky gets a queer gray. This is a sign that this bird is coming.

Coyote used to mock everything. If the birds had feathers, he wanted feathers. Everything that they could do, he wanted to do also.

They made each bird so that it had its own kind of feathers and looked different from the other birds. The black crow then was a pretty, white bird, but they hung him to a pine tree, smoked him, and made him black. Wood Rat had a song. Coyote used to urge him to sing it. He would tell him he had a good song and urge him to sing it again.

—Archup
(Stella LaRose, translator)

True Story

When Janie was about five year old, her father, her mother, and her mother's brother went hunting. Janie said to her father, "Let me ride with you behind," and she cried. Her mother said, "Don't let her go," but she cried to go. Then her father said, "Let her go," and he took her up behind.

They were going to get salt. Janie said, "Let me get off and get salt." Janie had on a little buckskin dress. She got off and she ran around and they had to chase her. She did not want to get up on the horse again. She put salt in her dress. George Ott [he is dead now] was a little boy then and he was along with his father.

While they were traveling they met some enemy. Janie's uncle said to her, "Get on the horse, all those Sioux coming. Get on quick!" Then her mother put her on her back and strapped her on. The Sioux were chasing antelope; there were lots of Sioux. The uncle said, "You didn't use your eyes. You thought those were just antelope, but they are Sioux."

Ute pass across the Rocky Mountains. Utes came down this trail to fight the Arapahoes and other plains peoples.

The Sioux came and caught up with them and killed all the women in the party except Janie and her mother. They heard lots of shouting over there. Janie and her family were away from the other bunch. If they had been with the big bunch, they would all have been killed too. The Sioux captured another woman, Kicica, and Janie and her mother. The Sioux tried to kill Kicica but her horse ran just like a racehorse. The Sioux followed Kicica and just surrounded Janie and her mother. They ran but the Sioux horses ran faster. Janie's uncle had medicine. The Sioux shot him but couldn't kill him. They could smell the smoke where the bullets hit, but they didn't hurt him. They were in a wash and the uncle dropped his medicine. The Sioux ammunition was gone now but they shot at him with arrows. He got an arrow in his side.

That little boy dropped from behind the saddle and hid in a hole and played dead. Then her uncle was mad. He said, "What are we going to do? I dropped my medicine." He had already killed two Sioux. They traveled a long ways, the Sioux after them. The Sioux took Kicica first, she had been scored by a bullet (a flesh wound) in her neck.

Janie and her mother had a lot of load on their horse and the mother said, "If I had a knife I could cut this and drop the load." She had a bridle with jingles; when they hit the horse on his face, it made him go. This day the horse didn't have this bridle on and the horse just stood, he wouldn't go. Two Sioux came up, one on each side and caught them. Janie and her mother were awful scared, they wouldn't talk. Some other Sioux came up leading Kicica on her horse.

Janie's father's sister had long, soft hair. She was going to have a baby and the Sioux shot her right where the baby was. The Sioux captured her mother's sister, her father's sister, Kicica, and Janie and her mother.

The Sioux said, "Shut your mouths, all of you. Don't talk," and the women kept quiet.

Janie's father had been in the battle. He had gone after a bunch of mules and horses the Sioux had. There were too many Sioux, they chased him. Her father's sister said, "Run, get away from those Sioux," and he ran and the Sioux chased him, but his horse was fast. It was an Arapaho racehorse. All the Sioux knew that horse, it was fast. Another man was with her father and they killed his horse and he got on double with Janie's father. An uncle (mother's brother) had hidden. In the afternoon her father and the man with him were looking from the top of the hill.

George Ott, when he was shot, ate a part of his medicine and he got all right. Another man who had medicine, the Sioux pounded and pounded, but they couldn't kill him.

Then they took the five captives away. The long-haired woman, she was a virgin, had tattoo marks on her cheek and forehead. Janie's mother was tattooed on the forehead. One woman said, "We might run away, we are not going to live over there."

In the evening Janie's father returned to the scene of the battle. All the dead were lying around. He couldn't find his wife. They must have taken her away.

The Sioux had also taken the pregnant woman (the shot didn't kill her, it went through buttocks).

The Sioux had taken all the meat the Utes were carrying.

After all the Sioux went away, George Ott, who had played dead, got up. His father had been wounded and lay down. George stayed with him. That evening he said, "Get up. All your friends are killed. I hear someone crying for his family. The Arapaho cry another way, it must be one of our people." It was Janie's father coming back. The boy said, "Maybe he will come to us and find us." The man said, "Get up where they can find you." The boy cried, "Oh, my uncle! All my sisters are gone with the Sioux, they took them away."

Janie's father and the man who had ridden double with him had gotten another horse. It belonged to a man who had been killed. They took George and his father up behind them on their horses.

The Sioux saw a pine that had been burned and they thought it was a man and tried to battle it.

The women and the Sioux traveled a long way east and

they got to where the Sioux lived. There were different bunches of Sioux. They stopped at that place. They found Ats, a Ute who had been captured a long time ago. He told Janie's mother, "That Sioux will take you for a wife, he has three wives now. I have a house up here." (That was just a joke. He was just trying to get her away.) The man who took Janie's mother for a wife was a bad man.

(Tufuv killed an Arapaho's son while he was asleep. "Did you see our boy?" he said to Tufuv. "No, I didn't see any boy.")

A Sioux boy traveled with Janie's mother and her husband. He was about twelve years old. He had to watch Janie's mother. A Sioux woman packed Janie. Janie's mother was pregnant by the Sioux. Then, when the Sioux were having a dance, one of the Sioux wives said to Janie's mother, "I'm going to let you go, let you have a saddle and everything."

Janie's father had tracked them to the Sioux place.

The Sioux quarrelled with his wife who was packing Janie. He said, "Let her down." The woman said, "Let us go to another Sioux place," and she took Janie and went.

The captured pregnant woman talked mad and they beat her. She was taken to a different bunch of Sioux than the other Ute captives.

The captured Ute said, "I live in a good place. Where you are going to live isn't a good place."

When the woman wanted to take Janie, Janie's mother said, "No, you're not going to take her. I don't want you to take my little girl. If you take my little girl, I won't be alive."

Close to their place that Sioux man got something to drink and he got drunk. They drank all night. He got money for drink by selling Janie's mother's mare. He fought with his wives then and threw them down on the ground. While he was drunk Janie's aunt ran away from the Sioux. He tied her wrist, but she worked the string loose and got away. She was the virgin. They raped her and she bled. The older wife said, "What's the matter, you open her, she bleed. There's something wrong to do that," and she fought with her husband.

The drunk man and his wives were left behind when the other Sioux went on. The long-haired woman escaped and ran away. She had nothing on her feet and she cut the sleeves of her buckskin dress and wrapped them around her feet.

All the Sioux were trying to cross a big river. It was deep and all the horses were jumping around. Janie's mother said, "What am I going to do?" The Sioux man had beaten one of his wives and she was crying. She said to Janie, "I have to make bread, lots of things for you to take with you. You got to run away from here back to your own people. I am going to turn you loose. I'll give you a saddle and bridle." Janie's mother said, "Don't sleep, we are going to travel." Janie said, "I'll look all night, I won't go to sleep. I'll go home to my father and my uncles."

Janie's mother was all ready—blanket, groceries, everything—when the Sioux came in and asked his wife, "Did you tie up that woman yet?" and she said, "Yes, I tied her up." So she covered her up with blankets. The Sioux put his hands on her feet to make sure she was there under the blanket, but he couldn't feel through the blanket that she wasn't tied. So he lay down and went to sleep and started snoring.

When he was asleep, his wife said to Janie's mother, "Take your blanket and your groceries and go out to the horse." That horse was a mean one and wouldn't let her get on. She said, "How am I going to get on?" It was a spotted horse. She tried to get on that horse. Then she finally got on that mean horse. Then somebody heard them. It was Pimpleface who heard them. Janie's mother heard later that the Sioux man beat his wife because she let Janie and her mother escape. This wife had a beautiful daughter and she used to tell her to take care of Janie. This woman also had another girl who used to tell Janie, "I'm going to whip you." She was mean.

Janie's mother said, "Let me catch this badger and I'll put it in the ashes," but she couldn't catch him, he ran fast. When they traveled they had to walk because that horse got lame and they left him someplace. That woman told them which way to go and where the Sioux were. When Janie's mother turned the horse loose, the Sioux got it and got all the groceries that were packed on it. They walked and they carried just a little of the groceries.

It rained. That time they made a bed out of bark. Her mother was sick, she was going to have a baby. They were near a road. Janie's mother said, "You go to that road and tell anybody, a white man maybe, I am sick. Maybe I'll die. You go and tell somebody to take you. I hurt. When that baby is born, I die."

That baby was born and she put her water bottle in the sun to get the water warm and she drank it up. Her mother gave the baby away to a white man they met on the way.

They were gathering salt at a big salt place in Colorado, white men have it now. [Impossible to get definite location.]

A Mexican told Janie's mother while they were traveling, "I saw a man who cried all the time. He has a mule and pack horse and he wears a buckskin suit. Maybe that is your man. He was traveling alone. I am going to kill a cow and give you some meat." Janie and her mother went home with the Mexican and they got something to eat.

That man who rode double with Janie's father spoke Mexican. When they got to where the Mexican who had fed Janie and her mother was, the Mexican told him, "I think I saw your woman. She got little baby." "No," said Janie's father, "my woman has just a little girl." But the Mexican described the woman and Janie's father said, "That is my woman." So, the Mexican told him where he had met Janie and her mother and they went and looked.

Janie's mother said to her, "You must think about this lots. You must have lots more sense now."

The white man to whom they gave the baby wrapped it in a coat and took it with him.

[The Sioux in this story were Arapaho.]

—Janie
(Mamie Alhandra, translator)

Another True Story

The reason the Arapaho could not shoot Archup's father was because he and a friend of his had the power so that they could not be hurt. It was their strong power, their strong belief that made them that way. It was just some kind of medicine they had in those days. Archup doesn't know what it was.

Then they captured some horses, they attacked the enemy. They went into the camps. The Arapaho were dancing and singing and did not know the Ute were there. They located the horses and drove them away with them. And then the enemy, when the Ute got away, heard the dogs bark and took out after them. So Archup's father and his friend said, "Let the other fellows go with the horses and we two will stay and give battle." Archup's father was on his best horse and they waited while the others went.

All the rest of the people had rushed to the mountains except those who came to fight the Utes and they fought all morning, until afternoon. The Utes' horses were shot from under them, but they kept on battling on foot. Finally, their ammunition ran out. More and more of the enemy kept coming and they got those fellows. They'd tried to kill them and they couldn't. Their knives wouldn't go through the flesh when they tried to stab them. They couldn't shoot them or stab them. The only way they finally got them was with rocks. They just pounded them to death. And after they were dead they just cut them all up into little pieces. They were so mad because the Utes had killed so many Arapaho. There was an old fellow on the mountain who watched the battle and his name was Tow sawuf^u. Archup knew him later and he showed Archup where this battle was. It was in Wyoming, in Arapaho country.

Tow sawuf^u came alone to White River after this battle. The fellows that took the horses had gone on ahead. Tow sawuf^u didn't catch up with them. He was scared.

The Arapaho moved camp and Tow sawuf^u went to their

old camp and saw these two friends of his who had been all
cut to pieces.

There was another fellow, a Ute, and he had lain in the
grass in the rushes and hid. He stayed hid until the Arapaho
had moved camp. He came back to White River, but he was
so poor, so worn out that when he finally reached a Ute camp
he had been hungry so long that when he ate, it killed him.

The old ones used to ask Archup if he could be like his
dad. He said he didn't know, he couldn't say. He never tired
himself out.

—ARCHUP

(Stella LaRose, translator)

The Captured Boy

Once the Comanche captured a little Ute boy. He grew up to
be a big man and when he got older he thought about himself
being a captured boy. Then he got acquainted with some of
the young boys there and there was one he liked real well.
And he said, "Let us go hunting and we will kill a buffalo and
make us some shields." So they went. They had four horses
that they took with them. They went to the Plains and they
staked their horses in the flats and they climbed a hill on foot.
They sat down and they saw some buffalo roaming around,
so the Comanche said, "Let's take a nap, I'm sleepy." The
Ute boy didn't go to sleep. He kept thinking. The other boy
was snoring in a little while. The Ute boy thought, "He is my
good friend, but this is my only chance to escape. I could kill
him and go back to my own people." So he got up and the
other boy still snored and the Ute boy got his gun and shot
his friend and killed him. He took his scalp and all his clothes
and made his getaway and came back to his own tribe.

When he came on the hill he saw some horses coming up
the river and he stopped and looked at them and he wondered how he was going to speak to his people and make
them understand. The boy left his other horses because he

wasn't sure whether these people he saw were Ute or not. He just took one horse. Then he saw one man coming afoot and he went and met him. The man was a Ute and they looked at each other and the boy asked, "Are you Ute?" He didn't know what else to say. The man said, "Yes, Ute," and patted his chest. He tried to make him understand that the Comanche had taken him when he was a little boy, he tried to talk by signs. The boy said, "Where is Kavita?" (He was a chief.)

The man took the boy to his camp and took him to one of the tipis there and said that was the chief's tent. They were curious to see the boy, and the man who brought him in said he thought he was a Ute boy. He was trying to explain his father's name to them, and his mother's name, but they did not understand. There was another bunch of people not far away and one man went and got someone who could speak other languages.

When this translator came, the boy told him how he had been captured and how he escaped. "Well," he said, "I've got some horses over there and all my friend's clothes." So the man went with him to get his stuff. When they got back the other band had come over to see if they could identify this kid. The translator told them all about the boy, but no one in that bunch could identify him. There was another bunch of people still farther away, so they sent a messenger over there to see if they could find the boy's mother. So they found an old lady who had lost her son and she came to see if he were her son. And she called him by the name she used to call her son and he found his mother.

They gave the mule that he had in his bunch of horses to the chief of the band he first met. He took the other horses and went with his mother's bunch. Then, after a while, he married a girl there.

He got hungry after a while and he wanted to go hunting. So they went after mountain sheep; he and his wife went. They made camp in the mountains beside a brook. Next morning he said, "I'm going hunting afoot. You stay here at camp." He got a ways away and looked back and saw a big fire there and he thought, "My wife is captured by somebody." When he got back there he saw a lot of horse tracks and his wife was gone. Then he had to go back all alone to his mother's camp.

He said, "I am going to search for my wife," but his mother did not want him to go. He insisted, and finally his mother said, "All right." He took his best horse and tracked the people who had taken his wife. He saw where they stayed overnight. When they got way far away, the tracks divided. Some went one way, some another. He followed those that went straight on. He followed them clear to where they were camped, so when he got there he saw some horses grazing. He stayed in the brush until it got dark.

In the evening a man took his horse to graze and the Ute met him and the enemy thought he was one of their own men and said, "Have you already put your horses out?" and the Ute replied, "Yes," and asked him, "What's going on?" The other man answered that some of the boys had just got back with an Indian woman they had captured and she was down in the camp. Everybody was going down to see her. "I'll go down with you," the man said, "if you will wait till I get my horses tended to." So the Ute said, "All right, hurry up."

He went and peeked in a tent and saw an old lady sitting with her back toward the fire. The old lady looked up and said, "Where have you been?" He said, "I've been hunting horses all day and I got home and nobody was there and I am hungry. Won't you cook me something to eat?" She got some meat and cooked it for him. While he was eating he asked for news. She told him about the captured Ute woman.

After he ate he went on. He saw a girl come out of a tent and go a little way and squat down. When she got up he grabbed her and she said, "Is that why you stayed?" And he said, "Yes, I knew you were alone and that is why I stayed." They went and copulated.

He got up very early in the morning and went toward the tent where the captured girl was. He met an old lady with a little girl riding behind. That old lady told him she had been to see the beautiful captive. Said they had a big dance. He had his bow and arrows and he shot that old lady under the ribs and killed her. She fell off the horse and the girl hollered. He took the little girl into the brush and tied her up and gagged her so that she couldn't holler. He waited there in the brush and at night he went nearer the tent where his wife was.

He sat in the brush near the tent and, while he was watching, he had got his horse. He could hear a drum and saw big fires starting up. He heard somebody talking. He crept closer and closer and heard someone behind him and saw it was the man he had met the day before. The other fellow said, "Oh, you beat me here." Together they crept a bit closer. Two other men came and said, "What are you two men doing here?" "Oh, just lying here. Where have they got that Ute girl?" "Oh, over in that tent there."

Then one said, "Let's go see her." So they went. When they got to the tent, the Ute said, "You go on in, I've got to go in the brush a minute. I'll come on in." So they went on ahead. The Ute gave a war whoop and the woman inside thought, "That sounds like my husband's voice." Then the Ute yelled again and the girl was sure that it was her husband. Then he yelled her name.

Nobody was right at the door when he came to it. He peeked in and saw his wife sitting next to a big man. She recognized him. Then he opened the door wider and she was sure it was her husband. She motioned toward where she slept. He went on back to the dance. The dance lasted until midnight and then the people went to their tents. Then he went back up to that tent. He got a rock and sharpened his knife.

Everybody got quiet after a while. He went sneaking behind the tipis, and the tent his wife was in was made of buffalo hides. He got to the place where she motioned she slept. On one side was an awful snorer. He began cutting at the tent, just made a slit in the tipi cover. The man just kept on snoring. The woman's hands were tied. He took his knife and cut the string. He gave her the knife and she cut the string around her ankles. Then she put her arms out through the hole and he pulled her out. Her new man was still snoring.

She told him where there were two good horses and they cut the ropes and got them. They led them by the tipis. When they passed the last tent an old man came out and yelled, "Ute!" but the Ute answered in the old man's language. "We're just taking the horses out to stake them." And the old man thought it was just a man and his wife. They went to where the man had left his horse staked and got that and then they went on home. They went to where he left that little girl tied in the brush and got the saddle from the old lady's horse. They took the little girl home with them.

[Archup says he used to hear his father tell this story often and he always treasured it; and now he tells it to me.]

—ARCHUP
(Stella LaRose, translator)

War Story

Long ago there was an enemy. The Ute attacked them. They kept just far enough away so they could make a hiding place. They had a sort of corner. Two or three days they kept them there and a brave man would go as near as he could and shoot at them. Then the brave man again would go and shoot another. Day and night, they guarded them.

Then after three or four days, when there were just a few left, they let them loose to try and let them get away if they could. But they shot at them as they ran. They just let one man of the enemy go so that he could tell the story. This rock cave where the enemy hid was down in southern Colorado. You can still see the holes where the arrows hit in the rock. The enemy were Comanche.

—ARCHUP
(Stella LaRose, translator)

Archup's Aunt

They were going on a journey, someplace back here, where they gather salt. She was riding on a pack horse that had two *parfleches* on it. While they were traveling, the Arapaho attacked them. They were going toward the place where they got salt. (The man who spoke was an old man with a little fellow riding behind him and they were going to get salt too.) That man told the woman to cut the strings that held the *parfleches* and to take the little boy behind her, and that would leave him free to battle the enemy. But she just kicked the horse and kept on going as hard as she could. She kept on and the man was fighting the enemy. This man was one of those fellows that couldn't be hit. He still had that little boy behind him and the enemy was shooting at them with bows and arrows. And when they got to some timber, he threw that little boy down and told him to hide under a log.

The enemy had circled them and when his aunt got through the timber, she found the enemy there, too, and they caught her. After the enemy caught this woman they went away, and then that man went back and got his boy from the timber where he was still hiding. [That boy used to tell Archup this story.]

There was another boy that they captured, too, and some other people. The girls got back and when they first captured them and took them to their camp they took a club and beat them. And the boy said in Ute, "They can't hit hard." And that woman said, "Haven't you got any sense? They have caught us and we'll never see our folks any more." And that boy thought about it and was sad and cried when they hit him. The man who captured a woman took her for a wife and she stayed there and learned their language. And this boy did this, too, and when he grew up he was just one of them. Later on, after his aunt had got used to their customs, she was all right. The man who captured her already had a wife, but he married her, too. Later on the man died. He had two boys by his first wife, and after he died there were just the four of them, the two kids and the two widows, and they always stayed together and traveled around together.

Whenever she would get the ribs to cook, she would just tear the meat off the bone with her mouth and the Arapaho woman wouldn't let her eat that way because that was just like scalping.

They traveled from the Arapaho camp to Wyoming, just going gradually, those two woman and kids. When they went one of the Arapaho women came to their tent and said, "Let's go swimming." There was a creek nearby. The Ute woman said, "All right, let's go." When they were swimming a white man came and the Ute woman jumped out and got her clothes on but the Arapaho stayed right in the water. Then this fellow said, "Are you the Indian woman I heard about? I am a white man, I'm a Mexican. There's going to be a dance in the town tonight and they'll feed the Indians." They had gotten a letter from Washington and knew this woman didn't belong to this tribe and they wanted to get her back to her own tribe.

The Arapaho woman asked what the white man said and the Ute woman said, "Oh, nothing. He just wanted to throw us down and copulate with us." Then next morning the chief was hollering, "Everybody get ready and get dressed up. There is going to be a dance in town." And the two boys told the old ladies to go and dance hard and earn a lot of crackers to bring home.

The ladies started and the two young Arapahos came along and one rode on each side of the Ute woman and said, "You don't belong here. Why don't you go back to your own home? It is not so far away." Then the Arapaho went away and the Ute woman caught up with her Arapaho woman friend who asked what the men said. The Ute woman said, "Oh, they just told us to dance hard."

When they got to town they saw white people all around. Then one of the boys came but he had forgotten his quiver, left it on his saddle, and he asked their mother to go get it and she said, "No, let the Ute woman get it." Then, when she got to the horse and reached for the quiver a white man grabbed her arm and said, "Come with me," and she went with him.

He took her upstairs in a house and told her to stay there. They were dancing outside and hollering that the Ute woman had disappeared. They thought she had run away. And she could hear them. They danced all afternoon and kept hollering, "Who saw the Ute woman?" She was still there all that time. Then she heard someone coming up after dark and the man came and said, "Hurry up." She went with him. And they got into a mail coach that was out there and they covered her up with the mail sacks. The kids thought she was in there and all hollered, "The Ute woman is in there."

Then they got to where they changed to fresh horses and they went on and did the same thing at the next station. The only station that she knew was at Denver. That is when she discovered where she was. She stayed there and they had a court and the translator was Mr. Curtis. A lot of people were in the court, and they said they wanted her back with her own people, with the Utes. Maybe she had a father or someone who needed her. The translator told her they were going to bring her back and she said, "If Washington says for me to go to my people, I'm willing to go if they will deliver me safe." So, they sent soldiers with her and lots of candy and stuff for her folks. They gave her a gray horse to ride, with saddle, bridle, everything. They said she could have them all, they were hers now.

They came to a town on the way back from Denver and all the soldiers got drunk and disappeared and the translator and the woman came on with all the mules and stuff. As they came along, Curtis said, "I think I better marry you," and she said, "They told me I was going to be delivered home safe. You didn't tell me anything about this." They came along and finally they got here and they went on to Salt Lake Valley.

The Indians were frightened and they thought it was a white man with an Indian wife and they wanted to kill the white man. The kids were all playing and they heard the men wanting to kill the man. But someone recognized her and called her name and she said, "Don't kill this man, he brought

me back safe to my people." They went to the chief and she
asked where her father's tipi was and he told her.

Sawamotatac (Blue Hummingbird) ran to his tent and
said, "That woman is back," and his mother said, "She can't
be—the Arapaho got her." Then she looked out and saw that
woman. Then they gave them the tobacco, cloth, and stuff
they had on the mules. Then Curtis took the mules back.

—ARCHUP

(Stella LaRose, translator)

History of the Utes

The time of this story is when Christ was on earth and the Indians at that time spoke one language or were of one nation.
They were camped east of the Rocky Mountains, on the
plains. The lodges could not be counted, there were so many
of them. At this time the entire nation of Indians were out of
meat, the women and children were crying, suffering from
starvation. The elders were asked by the other people to go
out and ask assistance from the Lord to help his people.

There were three of the elders that went out and there
were nine that remained at the camps to keep faith with the
people. They prayed the first day to the Father, without any
results. The second day they prayed, without any results.
The third day they were rewarded about the eighth or ninth
hour. They received instructions from the voice that came
out of a burning bush or mound. "I am He who will give you
meat if you will obey my rule or order. Go back to your
camps and open a way from the setting of the sun to the rising of the sun. I am your Father and I feed my children. I will
send you buffalo, elk, deer, and antelope. Get into line and
those that like buffalo all get into line by themselves, and so
on. Each family is to take their choice; one buffalo, one elk,
two deer, or two antelope. If they take more than this, the
meat will turn to worms and there will be a curse on the family that does it."

The record shows that there were some that disobeyed, and the following morning their meat was turned to worms. The ones that disobeyed were taken out and stoned. They fought and quarreled and even their language became so confused that they couldn't understand each other.

[From father to son, from son to son, handed down to the present time.]

—TECUMSEH MURRAY
(Josephine LaRose, translator)

How the Utes Got Land

Eighteen thirty-two, William Clark came through this country south of Denver. There were ten bands of Indians there. Three bands were Utes and these Utes whipped the other bands and retained their hunting grounds. The battleground was what they called the Lily Park Meadow. The armies assembled about a mile in length. There were about three thousand Utes and about five thousand of the other Indians. War chiefs met from each side. They were half a day deciding the way and time that they should fight. There were three white men as witnesses to their agreement. They agreed to leave the women and children a half day back from the fighting line.

The battle lasted three days and three nights. On the fourth morning the Utes were victorious, and the others had drawn away into the night. The Utes were there ten days, taking care of the wounded and burying the dead. Their wounded enemies were taken care of until they were well, and then they were allowed to return home when they were well. That is how the Utes became owners of the land from Denver to Salt Lake, through that war. They won it from the other seven tribes. Clark continued his journey to Sacramento, California, and returned to Washington, D.C., the following year.

—TECUMSEH MURRAY
(Josephine LaRose, translator)